MAXnotes®

Dante's
The Divine Comedy I: Inferno

Text by
Dr. Anita Price Davis
(Ed.D., Duke University)
Department of Education
Converse College
Spartanburg, South Carolina

Illustrations by
Karen Pica

REA *Research & Education Association*
Dr. M. Fogiel, Director

MAXnotes® for
THE DIVINE COMEDY I: INFERNO

Copyright © 2001, 1996 by Research & Education Association. All rights reserved. No part of this book may be reproduced in any form without permission of the publisher.

Printed in the United States of America

Library of Congress Control Number 00-108851

International Standard Book Number 0-87891-991-0

MAXnotes® is a registered trademark of Research & Education Association, Piscataway, New Jersey 08854

What **MAXnotes**® *Will Do for You*

This book is intended to help you absorb the essential contents and features of Dante's *The Divine Comedy I: Inferno* and to help you gain a thorough understanding of the work. Our book has been designed to do this more quickly and effectively than any other study guide.

For best results, this **MAXnotes** book should be used as a companion to the actual work, not instead of it. The interaction between the two will greatly benefit you.

To help you in your studies, this book presents the most up-to-date interpretations of every section of the actual work, followed by questions and fully explained answers that will enable you to analyze the material critically. The questions also will help you to test your understanding of the work and will prepare you for discussions and exams.

Meaningful illustrations are included to further enhance your understanding and enjoyment of the literary work. The illustrations are designed to place you into the mood and spirit of the work's settings.

The **MAXnotes** also include summaries, character lists, explanations of plot, and section-by-section analyses. A biography of the author and discussion of the work's historical context will help you put this literary piece into the proper framework of what is taking place.

The use of this study guide will save you the hours of preparation time that would ordinarily be required to arrive at a complete grasp of this work of literature. You will be well prepared for classroom discussions, homework, and exams. The guidelines that are included for writing papers and reports on various topics will prepare you for any added work which may be assigned.

The **MAXnotes** will take your grades "to the max."

Dr. Max Fogiel
Program Director

Contents

Section One: *Introduction* 1
   The Life and Work of Dante Alighieri 1
   Historical Background 2
   Master List of Characters 3
   Summary of the Work 9
   An Explanation of Dante's Hell 10
   Estimated Reading Time 11

Each canto includes List of Characters, Summary, Analysis, Study Questions and Answers, and Suggested Essay Topics.

Section Two:
The Comedy of Dante Alighieri Cantica I: Hell 12
   Canto I 12
   Canto II 16
   Canto III 19
   Canto IV 23
   Canto V 27
   Canto VI 31
   Canto VII 34
   Canto VIII 37
   Canto IX 41
   Canto X 46
   Canto XI 49

Canto XII 52
Canto XIII 56
Canto XIV 60
Canto XV 64
Canto XVI 66
Canto XVII 69
Canto XVIII 71
Canto XIX 74
Canto XX 78
Canto XXI 81
Canto XXII 85
Canto XXIII 87
Canto XXIV 91
Canto XXV 93
Canto XXVI 98
Canto XXVII 102
Canto XXVIII 105
Canto XXIX 108
Canto XXX 111
Canto XXXI 114
Canto XXXII 117
Canto XXXIII 121
Canto XXXIV 125

Section Three: *Sample Analytical Paper Topics* 130

Section Four: *Bibliography* 137

A Glance at Some of the Characters

Dante

Cerberus

Chiron

Virgil

Judas Iscariot

Medusa

Beatrice

Three Furies

SECTION ONE

Introduction

The Life and Work of Dante Alighieri

Dante Alighieri, the son of a nobleman, was born in May of 1265 in Florence, Italy. Dante received his early education in Florence but later attended the University of Bologna. His learning experiences included a tour in the Florence army when he fought at the Battle of Campaldino.

Dante's great love seems to have been Beatrice—probably Beatrice Portinari. Dante and Beatrice met when they were children and Dante apparently worshipped her. Beatrice was Dante's inspiration for *The Divine Comedy*; after her death in 1290, he dedicated a memorial "The New Life" (*La Vita Nuova*) to her. Though each married, they did not marry each other.

Dante instead entered an arranged marriage in 1291 with Gemma Donati, a noblewoman; they had two sons and either one or two daughters. Records contain little else about their life together.

By 1302 Dante was a political exile from Florence. He probably started *The Divine Comedy* after this exile. Politics, history, mythology, religious leaders, and prominent people of the time, of literature, of the past, and of Dante's personal life—including Beatrice—appear throughout *The Divine Comedy*. The work was a major departure from most of the literature of the day since it was written in Italian, not the Latin of most other important writing. Dante finished *The Divine Comedy* just before his death on September 14, 1321; he was still in exile and was living under the protection of Guido da Polenta in Ravenna. Perhaps still bitter from his expulsion from Florence, Dante wrote on the title page of *The Divine Comedy* that he was "a Florentine by birth, but not in manner" (Bergin, 444).

Bergin describes Dante as "the first important writer to emerge after the Dark Ages" and his work as "the beginning of the Italian Renaissance in literature" (444). According to Bergin, "*The Divine Comedy* is a complete expression of medieval philosophy, religion, and culture. The beauty of its poetry and the universality of its scope [especially in this time when distractions abound] make it one of the most sublime achievements in all literature" (444). While some found fault with a writer who put those with whom he differed in Hell and those whom he favored in Heaven (Vincent), many critics of the day heaped praise on the work which reflected the religious outlook of an earlier day and yet contained the robust language of the Italian people along with vivid imagery. Other Italian writers, such as Petrarch and Boccaccio, used Dante's work as a model—the most sincere form of flattery.

Historical Background

The Renaissance, or the rebirth of learning, began in Italy in the fourteenth century and influenced all of Western civilization. Wealthy families in Italy, such as the Medicis of Florence, were patrons of the arts and sciences. Trade flourished and prosperity thrived throughout much of the country.

In contrast to these positive occurrences, all was not well in Italy during the Renaissance. Rulers of the independent Italian states often fought with each other to establish a large political unit. The Guelph Political party (which favored local authority) and the Ghibelline Political party (which favored imperial authority) were two such rival factions; the two had been at war periodically since the thirteenth century.

Dante's birth in 1265 came at a time when the Guelph party, favoring local authority, was in control of Florence. Dante turned away from his Guelph heritage to embrace the imperial philosophy of the Ghibellines. His change in politics is best summed up in his treatise *De Monarchia*, in which Dante states his belief in the separation of church and state. The Ghibellines, however, were pushed from power by the Guelphs during Dante's adulthood and confined to northern Tuscany.

Introduction

The Guelph Political party eventually divided into two groups: the Whites (led by the Cerchi family) and the Blacks (led by the Donati family and later aided by Pope Boniface VIII). Dante became a member of the Whites and served as an ambassador to talk with the Pope in Rome about conditions in Florence. While Dante was out of town, the Blacks took over Florence. The Blacks sentenced Dante to banishment from the city; his punishment for return would be death. His wanderings gave him time to write and to study the Scriptures. This banishment also gave Dante his perspective on the corruption of the fourteenth century papacy, a view that he would clearly describe in *The Inferno*.

In the year 1310, Henry VII became Holy Roman Emperor; Dante believed that this German prince would bring peace. But Henry VII died in 1313 and his Italian campaign collapsed. Dante became disillusioned and left the political life; he ceased work on other materials he had begun and concentrated on *The Divine Comedy*.

Master List of Characters

Note: The Canto in which the characters first appear is listed after their names.

Dante (Canto I)—*The writer, narrator, main character, and traveler in* The Inferno

Virgil (Canto I)—*Ancient Roman poet who appears to Dante and becomes his guide*

Aeneas (Canto II)—*A character from Virgil's Aeneid; "author of young Silvius' birth"*

Alessio Interminei (Canto XVIII)—*A White Guelph; a flatterer with "slick" manners*

Alexandro degli Alberto (Canto XXXII)—*One of two shades in Region i, Circle IX; one of the brothers who slew one another in a fight over family land*

Antaeus (Canto XXXI)—*One of the giants visible from the waist up above the rim of the well; he is invincible on earth but not in the air or sky; carries Virgil and Dante to the pit bottom*

Aretine (Canto XXIX)—*Griffolino d'Arezza; a physicist; took money for promising miracles; burned at stake for falsifying*

Barrators (Canto XXI)—*Sinners who made money in public office*

Beatrice (Canto II)—*Woman who begs Virgil to rescue Dante (Heavenly Wisdom)*

Bertrand de Born (Canto XXVIII)—*Headless shade who helped increase feud between Henry II of England and his young son Prince Henry*

Blasphemers (Canto XIV)—*Includes Capaneus, one of seven kings in siege of Thebes*

Bocca degli Abati (Canto XXXII)—*Ghibelline; fought on the Guelph side in the Battle of Montaperti; cut off the hand of the man who carried the standard*

Brutus (Canto XXXIV)—*Opposed to the Divine and secular world; a resident of Dis*

Buoso da Duera (Canto XXV)—*Commander of the Ghibellines; sold passage to the opposing French army and was, therefore, a traitor to his country*

Cacus (Canto XXV)—*Dragon with spread wings and breath of fire*

Caiaphas (Canto XXIII)—*High priest; condemned Christ; crucified in Hell by triple stake*

Camicion de' Pazzi (Canto XXXII)—*Introduced shades to Dante in Region i, Circle IX; quick to identify other wrong-doers; less-likely to identify own wrongs; murdered Ubertino, his own kinsman*

Capocchio (Canto XXIX)—*Student with Dante; an alchemist who called self an "ape of nature" because of his power to mimic or to produce a draught*

Carlino dei Pazzi (Canto XXXII)—*Bribed by Blacks to surrender the castle he was holding for the Whites; later sold castle to Whites again*

Cassius (Canto XXXIV)—*Defeated by Anthony and took his own life; a resident of Dis*

Introduction

Catalano and Loderingo (Canto XXIII)—*Two hooded friars from Bologna*

Cavalcante dei Cavalcanti (Canto X)—*A shade who was once of the Guelph party*

Centaurs (Canto XII)—*Creatures with the heads of men and the bodies of horses*

Cerberus (Canto VI)—*The three-headed dog of Hell; watches over the Third Circle*

Charon (Canto III)—*The white-haired boat keeper who takes travelers across the Acheron River*

Chiron (Canto XII)—*Chief centaur*

Ciacco (Canto VI)—*Gluttonous male inhabitant of Florence; nickname means "pig"*

Curio (Canto XXVIII)—*Brought about civil strife; tongue removed for punishment*

Deianira (Canto XII)—*Wife of Hercules; dipped his shirt in blood of Nessus*

Demons (Canto XXI)—*Include Hacklespur, Hellkin, Harrowhound, Libbicock, Dragonel, Barbinger, Grabbersnitch, Rubicant, Farfarel, Belzecue*

Diomede (Canto XXVI)—*Half of The Dual Flame; planned the Trojan horse with Ulysses*

Dis (Canto XXIV)—*Satan; ruler of the pit*

Ephialtes (Canto XXXI)—*One of the giants visible from the waist up above the rim of the well; Ephialtes attacked Jove*

The False Wife (Canto XXX)—*Reference to the wife of Potiphar (Book of Genesis); tries to lie with Joseph and, when he refuses, falsely accuses him*

Farinata degli Uberti (Canto X)—*Leader of the Ghibellines, the party responsible for killing Dante's grandfather; favored imperial authority*

Filippo Argenti (Canto VIII)—*Florentine resident; had differed politically with Dante*

Five Spirits (Canto XXV)—*Florentine noblemen who (except for Puccio) change to animal shapes; include Agnello dei Brunelleschi, Cianfa die Donate, Buoso Degli Abati, Francesco Guercio dei Cavalcanti, and Puccio dei Galigai*

Francesca and Paolo (Canto V)—*Adulterous couple killed by Francesca's husband, Gian Ciotto*

Friar Alberigo (Canto XXXIII)—*Soul in Patolomaea, where traitors and their guests reside*

Geryon (Canto XVII)—*The monster from the Circles of Fraud; also a monster killed by Hercules; part beast, part man, and part reptile*

Gianni Schicchi (Canto XXX)—*Falsifier who dressed as Buoso and dictated a new will*

Guido, Alexander, and their Brother (Canto XXX)—*Blamed for Adam's counterfeiting; part of the Conti Guidi family*

Guido da Montefeltro (Canto XXVII)—*Ghibelline leader who persuaded Pope Boniface VIII to use treachery to gain the fortress of Palestrina*

Harpies (Canto XIII)—*Voracious creatures with bodies of birds and heads of women*

The Heavenly Messenger (Canto IX)—*Helper to Virgil and Dante; possibly St. Paul*

The Heretics (Canto IX)—*In open graves; had trusted reason rather than the church*

Horned Fiends (Canto XVIII)—*Those who beat the naked sinners in the Malbowges*

Hypocrites (Canto XXIII)—*Wear cloaks with hoods, bright colors, and lead linings*

Jason (Canto XVIII)—*Greek hero who searched for the golden fleece and seduced others*

Judas Iscariot (Canto XXXIV)—*Betrayer of Jesus*

Leopard (Canto I)—*The first character (Self-indulgence) whom Dante meets*

Introduction

Lion (Canto I)—*The second character (Violence) whom Dante meets*

Mahomet (Canto XXVIII)—*Seen by Dante and Virgil; Italian spelling of Mohammed, founder of Islam*

Master Adam (Canto XXX)—*Counterfeited Romena coins bearing John the Baptist*

Medusa (Canto IX)—*Evil, serpent-haired goddess; could turn people to stone*

Minos (Canto V)—*Legendary King of Crete who occupies the threshold of the Second Circle and assigns places to the damned*

Minotaur (Canto XII)—*Creature with the head of a bull and the body of a man*

Mosca (Canto XXVIII)—*Brought Florentine division by creating Guelphs and Ghibellines*

Myrrha (Canto XXX)—*According to Ovid, disguised self and was impregnated by own father (King of Cyprus); turned into a myrtle tree and bore Adonis—a son—through the bark*

Napoleone (Canto XXXII)—*One of two shades in Region i, Circle IX; one of the brothers whom slew one another in a fight over family land*

Nessus (Canto XII)—*Centaur who tried to carry off Deianira (wife of Hercules); his blood on Hercules's shirt caused Hercules so much pain that Hercules burned himself to death*

Nimrod (Canto XXXI)—*One of the giants visible from the waist up above the rim of the well; loosed the bands of common speech*

Phlegyas (Canto VIII)—*The mariner on the Styx who comes for Dante and Virgil*

Pier da Medicina (Canto XXVIII)—*Incited civil strife; disseminated scandal and misrepresentation; incited feuds between two Romagna families*

Pier delle Vigne (Canto XIII)—*Accused of plotting against Fredrick II; took own life after being blinded and imprisoned; deemed guilty of only suicide—not betrayal—by Dante since in upper level*

Pluto (Canto VII)—*God of the underworld; at entrance to the Fourth Circle*

Ruggieri degli Ubaldini (Canto XXXIII)—*Archbishop who imprisoned Count Ugolino*

St. Lucia (Canto II)—*Messenger from the Virgin Mary*

St. Paul (Canto II)—*One who, like Dante, writes of his view of Hell*

Sassol Mascheroni (Canto XXXII)—*In Region i, Circle IX; murdered uncle's only son (Sassol's cousin) and took the inheritance.*

Ser Branca d' Oria (Canto XXXIII)—*Shade waiting in Patolomaea until years of his body are up*

She-Wolf (Canto I)—*The third character (Malice) whom Dante meets*

Simoniacs (Canto XIX)—*Include Pope Nicholas III; profited from sale of holy items*

Sinon of Troy (Canto XXX)—*Greek spy who persuaded the Trojans to bring the wooden horse into the gates of Troy*

The Soul from Navarre (Canto XXII)—*Probably Gian Polo; Spaniard; former servant*

Three Florentines (Canto XVI)—*Ask Dante about Florence; now in Hell*

Three Furies (Canto IX)—*Queen Medusa's handmaids: Alecto, Magaera, Tisiphone*

"Two that ran" (Canto XIII)—*A reference to Lano of Siena (who sold his estates with other young men in a club and who wasted his money and life) and to Jacomo di Sant Andrea (who burned his own home for fun)*

Ugolino della Gherardesca (Canto XXXIII)—*Guelph leader who ate human flesh; imprisoned in the Tower of Famine; saw sons and grandsons starve*

Ulysses (Canto XXVI)—*Half of the Dual Flame; planned the Trojan horse with Diomede*

Vanni Fucci from Pistoia (Canto XXIV)—*A thief; a runner from the serpents in the trench; predicts the future to hurt Dante*

Introduction

Venedico Caccianemico (Canto XVIII)—*Member of the Guelphs who sold his own sister*

Violent Sinners (Canto XII)—*Guilty of violence, included Pyrrhus, Achilles' cruel son*

The Virgin Mary (Canto I)—*Sends the messenger St. Lucia to Virgil*

Summary of the Work

The Divine Comedy is a narrative poem describing Dante's imaginary journey. Midway on his journey through life, Dante realizes he has taken the wrong path. The Roman poet Virgil searches for the lost Dante at the request of Beatrice; he finds Dante in the woods on the evening of Good Friday in the year 1300 and serves as a guide as Dante begins his religious pilgrimage to find God. To reach his goal, Dante passes through Hell, Purgatory, and Paradise.

The Divine Comedy was not titled as such by Dante; his title for the work was simply *Commedia* or *Comedy*. Dante's use of the word "comedy" is medieval by definition. To Dante and his contemporaries, the term "comedy" meant a tale with a happy ending, not a funny story as the word has since come to mean.

The Divine Comedy is made up of three parts, corresponding with Dante's three journeys: *Inferno*, or "Hell"; *Purgatorio*, or "Purgatory"; and *Paradiso*, or "Paradise." Each part consists of a prologue and approximately 33 cantos. Since the narrative poem is in an exalted form with a hero as its subject, it is an epic poem.

Dante and Virgil enter the wide gates of Hell and descend through the nine circles of Hell. In each circle they see sinners being punished for their sins on earth; Dante sees the torture as Divine justice. The sinners in the circles include:

Circle One - Those in limbo
Circle Two - The lustful
Circle Three - The gluttonous
Circle Four - The hoarders
Circle Five - The wrathful
Circle Six - The heretics
Circle Seven - The violent

  Ring 1. Murderers, robbers, and plunderers
  Ring 2. Suicides and those harmful to the world
  Ring 3. Those harmful against God, nature, and art, as well as usurers
 Circle Eight - The Fraudulent
  Bowge (Trench) I. Panderers and Seducers
  Bowge II. Flatterers
  Bowge III. Simoniacs
  Bowge IV. Sorcerers
  Bowge V. Barrators
  Bowge VI. Hypocrites
  Bowge VII. Thieves
  Bowge VIII. Counselors
  Bowge IX. Sowers of Discord
  Bowge X. Falsifiers
 Circle Nine - Traitors
  Region i: Traitors to their kindred
  Region ii: Traitors to their country
  Region iii: Traitors to their guests
  Region iv: Traitors to their lords

On Easter Sunday, Dante emerges from Hell. Through his travels, he has found his way to God and is able, once more, to look upon the stars.

An Explanation of Dante's Hell

A reader encountering *The Inferno* without any prior knowledge of the relationship between the Greek and Roman cultures can easily be confused by Dante's design of Hell. In the upper circles of Hell, Dante has placed characters whose sins included lust, wrath, and violence; in the lower, more evil circles are sinners who lied, deceived, and committed treason. To modern-day readers, this categorization of evils may seem backwards, but Dante's Hell is consistent with Roman thought.

The Romans adopted almost their entire civilization from the Greeks, except their notion of sin. The Greeks felt that a violent act against another human being was the worst form of evil. A good example is the Trojan Horse in Homer's *The Iliad*. The Greeks

Introduction

exalted the resourcefulness and inventiveness of the Trojan Horse. The Roman idiom hated the Trojan Horse for its deceitfulness. The Romans held deceit and treason as the worst of all evils and felt physical violence was not as harsh. This belief could stem from the fact that the Roman Empire was so strong that it had nothing to fear from physical violence but was always defeated by treason and treachery.

Dante believed in the Roman idea of evil, so his structure of Hell is consistent. There are lesser examples of Dante's affection for Roman culture, such as his spelling "Odysseus" with its Latin form, "Ulysses." Although it may not fit contemporary views of evil, Dante's Hell is consistent with the Roman ideas of sin.

Estimated Reading Time

The average silent reading rate for a secondary student is 250 to 300 words per minute. Since each page contains approximately 11 stanzas of 27 words, the average number of words per page is 300 words. The words in Dante's *Inferno* include many which most students have never heard or seen; since these words relate to the geography of a foreign country, people who are not well-known, and lesser mythological characters, students should adjust their reading rate accordingly. Since it is important that students consult the endnotes, glossary, and/or a dictionary, the reading rate will be slowed further.

Each page takes readers 2-3 minutes if they read carefully, consult the notes in the edition they are reading, use the dictionary or glossary regularly, and take notes for study purposes. Since there are 291 pages in the *Penguin Classics* edition, this means that the student will need 291 times 3 minutes, or 873 minutes (about 15 hours). It is evident, then, that the estimated reading time for this book is longer than for a typical narrative. Reading *The Inferno* according to the natural canto breaks is the best approach.

SECTION TWO

The Comedy of Dante Alighieri
Cantica I: Hell

Canto I

New Characters:

Dante: *The writer, narrator, main character, and traveler in* The Inferno

Leopard: *The first character (Self-indulgence) whom Dante meets*

Lion: *The second character (Violence) whom Dante meets*

She-Wolf: *The third character (Malice) whom Dante meets*

Virgil: *Ancient Roman poet who appears to Dante and becomes his guide*

Summary

Midway on his journey through life, Dante falls asleep and loses his way. He wakes during the night of Maundy Thursday to find himself in a dark wood; he does not know how he got there. Dante loses the right way; the narrow road he had wanted to travel has disappeared. Dante feels hope when he sees the morning rays of sun over the mountain, even though he is still alone in the valley.

Canto I

As he scales the mountain, Dante encounters a leopard; the leopard impedes his progress but it is not very frightening. The second animal that Dante meets is a fierce, hungry lion, which comes toward him swiftly and savagely. The third—and worst—animal that Dante encounters is a vicious she-wolf; she terrifies Dante so much that he is unable to continue his travels.

The shade of the poet Virgil appears to Dante. Until the greyhound comes to secure the wolf in Hell, Virgil explains, the only way past the wolf is by another path. Virgil offers to show Dante the path to an eternal place where he can see long-parted souls; at that point, Virgil says, another guide will come and take Dante to a city which Virgil cannot enter. Dante accepts Virgil's offer and follows the poet.

Analysis

Dante has lost the narrow way to God; he finds himself in a dark forest in the valley of sin and separation from God. Dante is not sure how he lost the bright, right, narrow way; the darkness of sin and night (Maundy Thursday before the Passover) frightens him. When Good Friday (the morning of Jesus's crucifixion) arrives, Dante feels hope as he sees the rays of light (goodness) shine over the mountain—a symbol of the ascent from evil that one must make to reach God.

The three animals—leopard, lion, and wolf—are images of sin. The first animal (the leopard) depicts the sins of self-indulgence or incontinence, which are often the sins of youth. The lion represents the sins of bestial violence which are often the sins of adulthood; the wolf symbolizes the malicious sins, the sins of age. The greyhound is a symbol of the political or religious leader who will come to help rid the world of greed; it could also symbolize Dante's friend Can Grande (Italian for "great dog") della Scala, the Ghibelline leader.

Virgil represents human reason, which can help—to a point—in bringing Dante out of the wood. Virgil was the inspiration for Dante; Virgil's *Aeneid* was the pattern for *The Inferno*. It is natural that Virgil should guide Dante when Dante was lost in life just as Virgil guided Dante as Dante wrote. Virgil's hoarseness could refer to his not having spoken since he began his journey into Hell or it could refer to the fact that he had not spoken to the world for some time since he was not a popular writer at the time. It is significant that Virgil cannot speak until Dante speaks to him.

From the beginning of Canto I, three main themes are evident. The first and most important of Dante's main themes is the picaresque (or journey) theme; Dante's journey to the nether regions is vital to *The Inferno*. With pilgrimages being common in the 1200s and 1300s and with the influence of Virgil's writings on Dante, it is not surprising that Dante uses the picaresque theme. A second theme in *The Inferno* is the survival of the unfittest; a weak, lost Dante encounters three wild animals and even manages a trip to the depths of Hell and back. A third main theme is the reversal of fortune; Dante is lost at the beginning of Canto I, but by the end of *The Inferno*, he has found his way.

Study Questions

1. What was Virgil's occupation? When and where did he live?
2. Where did Virgil tell Dante that joy and its beginning could be found?
3. Name the creatures that Dante finds in the woods.
4. Which creature was the most horrible and why?
5. Dante felt fear for many reasons. What were some of these reasons?
6. Why did Dante not know how he got into the woods?
7. What helped Dante to feel hope?
8. What did Virgil say they would see and hear on the journey?
9. Why did Virgil explain that some sufferers were happy in their pain?
10. Virgil said he would guide Dante on a journey but Virgil would have to turn back at one point. Where would Virgil stop with Dante?

Canto I

Answers

1. Virgil was a poet in ancient Rome.
2. Virgil told Dante that joy and its beginning could be found on the mountain.
3. Dante finds a leopard, a lion, and a wolf in the woods.
4. The wolf was the most horrible since it was greedy and never satisfied; it represented sins of age.
5. Dante felt fear from being lost, from being in the woods, from the three creatures he saw, and from the darkness of sin and the night.
6. Dante became lost because he was not paying attention; he strayed farther and farther before he became aware of his errors. He was lost in sin and lost in the dark valley.
7. Dante felt hope when he saw the sun and encountered Virgil. Dante's hope was increased when Virgil said that he would serve as Dante's guide.
8. Virgil said they would gaze on those in the fire and hear the despairing cries of those in the pit before Dante would climb higher.
9. Some sufferers were happy to be in pain for they looked forward to rising ultimately to a glad place.
10. Virgil would turn back at the gates of Heaven.

Suggested Essay Topics

1. Dante uses several symbols for sin and righteousness in Canto I. What are the representations? Which do you think is the most effective and why?
2. Compare and contrast the sins of youth, adulthood, and age.

Canto II

New Characters:

Beatrice: *Woman who begs Virgil to rescue Dante (Heavenly Wisdom)*

St. Lucia: *Messenger from the Virgin Mary*

The Virgin Mary: *Sends the messenger St. Lucia to Virgil*

Aeneas: *A character from Virgil's Aeneid; author of "young Silvius' birth"*

St. Paul: *One who, like Dante, writes of his view of Hell*

Summary

Friday has almost ended. Dante and Virgil have been climbing most of the day. Dante begins to question whether he should continue the journey. Dante remembers that Aeneas and St. Paul traveled to Hell and he feels inferior to both of them. Dante asks who said he should go to this place and what would happen if he should fail.

Virgil tells him that an angelic spirit named Beatrice had concern for Dante. The Virgin Mary sent Beatrice to Virgil through St. Lucia, her messenger, to ask Virgil to bring Dante from his wandering.

Virgil tells Dante to be brave; three women in Heaven are concerned for him. Dante confesses that his courage is now stronger. Virgil moves on and Dante follows him.

Analysis

Aeneas was a Trojan prince and the hero of *Aeneid*, written by Virgil. In *Aeneid*, Aeneas, the father of Silvius, goes to Hades, guided by the Sibyl, and returns safely; while there, he visits his father Anchises and learns that he is to be the ancestor of the Romans. St. Paul also visits Hell through a vision. Dante feels inferior to St. Paul and the great writer Virgil; yet he, too, is getting ready to

Canto II

make the journey to view Hell. This journey may be the one that the main character Dante will make, but it may also be a reference to the journey that Dante the writer will make as he records *The Inferno* on paper. Dante is probably comparing himself unfavorably with St. Paul, Virgil, and Aeneas and comparing his writing skills unfavorably with those of St. Paul and Virgil.

Virgil tells Dante how the Virgin Mary, the messenger St. Lucia, and Beatrice had concern for Dante. Mary is the vessel of Divine Grace; her name and the name of Christ are never spoken in Hell. St. Lucia is the patron saint of those with weak sight; it is appropriate that her name be mentioned since Dante has been lost. The third image of Divine Grace is Beatrice, a woman whom Dante had known since he was 9 and she was 8; even though Beatrice married another, Dante never ceased to love her. Beatrice died in 1290 at the age of 27. The character of Beatrice is a reference to this sacred love of Dante's life; her very existence is a reminder to Dante of the presence of God. Throughout *The Inferno* no one ever mentions either her name or the name of Christ in Hell; their names are too sacred to be profaned by their mere mention in Hell.

Virgil's story causes Dante's courage to blossom as a flower, and they are able to continue their journey in confidence.

Study Questions

1. With which two other travelers does Dante compare himself unfavorably?
2. Who opposes cruelty?
3. What is Virgil's impression of Dante's courage?
4. What happens to Dante's courage after Virgil talks to him?
5. Who was the heavenly woman who was concerned about Dante?
6. Who was the New Testament Saint who recorded his images of Hell?
7. Who created the character of Aeneas?
8. Who guarded the gates of Heaven?
9. How does Virgil's courage compare to Dante's?

10. Why did Virgil decide to try to rescue Dante from his wanderings?

Answers
1. Dante compares himself unfavorably with the travelers St. Peter and Aeneas.
2. Lucy (St. Lucia) opposes cruelty of every kind.
3. Virgil sees Dante as a coward.
4. Dante's courage blossoms like a flower after Virgil talks with him.
5. Beatrice was very concerned about Dante.
6. Paul was the New Testament Saint who recorded his images of Hell.
7. Aeneas was the character created by Virgil.
8. St. Peter guarded the gates of Heaven.
9. Virgil's courage is initially great in comparison to Dante's.
10. Beatrice and St. Lucia, the messenger of the Virgin Mary, talked him into the rescue.

Suggested Essay Topics
1. Dante compares himself to others who visited the world of Hades. Who were these persons and why did they make the journey? How would their journeys have affected Dante's confidence in his completing the upcoming journey?
2. What kinds of love are evident in Canto II? Explain your answer.

Canto III

New Characters:

Uncommitted: *Souls not rebellious against God and yet not committed*

Charon: *One who takes travelers across the Acheron River*

Summary

Dante and Virgil pass through the wide gates of Hell. They read the inscription there ("Abandon hope, all ye who enter here.") and enter the Vestibule of Hell. They see those who were true only to themselves in their prior life; these people were not rebellious against God and yet they were not committed to Him in their life on earth. These people rush about but never make any decision; their faces bleed from the sting and bite of hornets and wasps and worms devour the blood which drips to the ground.

Virgil and Dante find a boat rowed by a white-haired man. This ferryman of the Acheron River reminds them that those who cross do not return; Virgil explains that one with will and power has deemed otherwise. When Dante hears the noise of the wind and sees the danger below, he swoons.

Analysis

The gates of Hell are wide and easy to enter; this is in direct contrast to the straight, narrow way that Dante lost before he found himself in the wood on Maundy Thursday. The inscription reminds those who enter that they must give up all hope; they make the trip to Hell as a choice and cannot return. This inscription, Virgil reminds him, does not apply to Dante. Dante is not dead and he has been given special permission to visit beyond the gates. Dante, nevertheless, feels fear; Virgil must smile and again remind Dante that the inscription does not include them at this time.

The uncommitted are the first souls that they encounter in Hell. These cowards have no hope of death (Hell) or life (Heaven) because they never made a decision for evil or good. Because they never shed their blood willingly for a cause, they now must shed it unwillingly. The loss counts for nothing now; the lowly worms devour their blood.

The journey to Hell is a conscious choice on the part of those who make the trip. The trip is not made by accident or because of just one error in life; rather the damned fear but desire Hell much as a sinner may hate their sin and yet continue to commit it. Dante

Canto III

is amazed by the number of uncommitted; the sights and sounds of Hell frighten him and Canto III ends as Dante swoons.

Study Questions
1. What was Dante's first reaction to the wailing?
2. To what does Dante compare the worry that the uncommitted might be missing something?
3. What is the name of the river which circles the rim of Hell?
4. What was the name of the ferryman?
5. Who were the *cowards* in Canto III?
6. The river's name is translated as "joyous." Why is this a good name for the river?
7. The uncommitted had saved their blood all their lives. What was the ultimate result of this act?
8. What is Dante's initial reaction to the many souls he sees in the Vestibule of Hell?
9. Who are the cowards whom Dante describes?
10. What is Dante's reaction to the sights and sounds of Hell at the end of Canto III?

Answers
1. Dante cried when he heard the sound of the wailing.
2. Dante compared the worry that the uncommitted might be missing something to the sting of wasps and bees.
3. The river was the Acheron.
4. The ferryman was named Charon.
5. The *cowards* are those who were afraid to make a decision.
6. The river could bring joy because it takes the dead to an area where they have made a conscious decision to travel.
7. They now find their blood spilled by wasps and hornets and drunk by worms.

8. Dante is surprised at their numbers; he had no idea so many had died or that so many had died uncommitted.
9. The cowards that Dante describes are the people who were not brave enough to make a decision one way or the other.
10. Dante is frightened and falls into a swoon.

Suggested Essay Topics
1. What is the crime of the uncommitted? What is their punishment? Is this penalty related to the crime? Explain your answer.
2. Why does Charon dispute taking Dante on his boat?

Canto IV

New Characters:

The Blameless but Unbaptized and Those Who Lived Before the Age of Christendom: *Souls in limbo from the First Circle*

Summary

Dante awakens to find that he is on the brink of Hell. When Dante looks into the pit, he cannot see its bottom. Virgil tells him that they must travel into the pit. Dante says that Virgil's pallor frightens him, but Virgil says it is the anguish within the pit and not the journey that causes his pallor.

From the First Circle come not the wails of anguish but the sounds of sighing. The souls which are sighing are those who are blameless but unbaptized and those who lived good lives before the time of Christendom. Dante asks if anyone had ever come from this circle and Virgil tells him that those who left were the first father (Adam), Abel (son of Adam), Noah (patriarch saved during the flood by heeding God's command to build an ark), Moses (leader who received the Ten Commandments), King David (King of Israel), Abraham (the father of Isaac), Israel (Jacob) with his father and generation, Rachel (mother of Joseph), and others. The one with a crown of victory removed these from the First Circle.

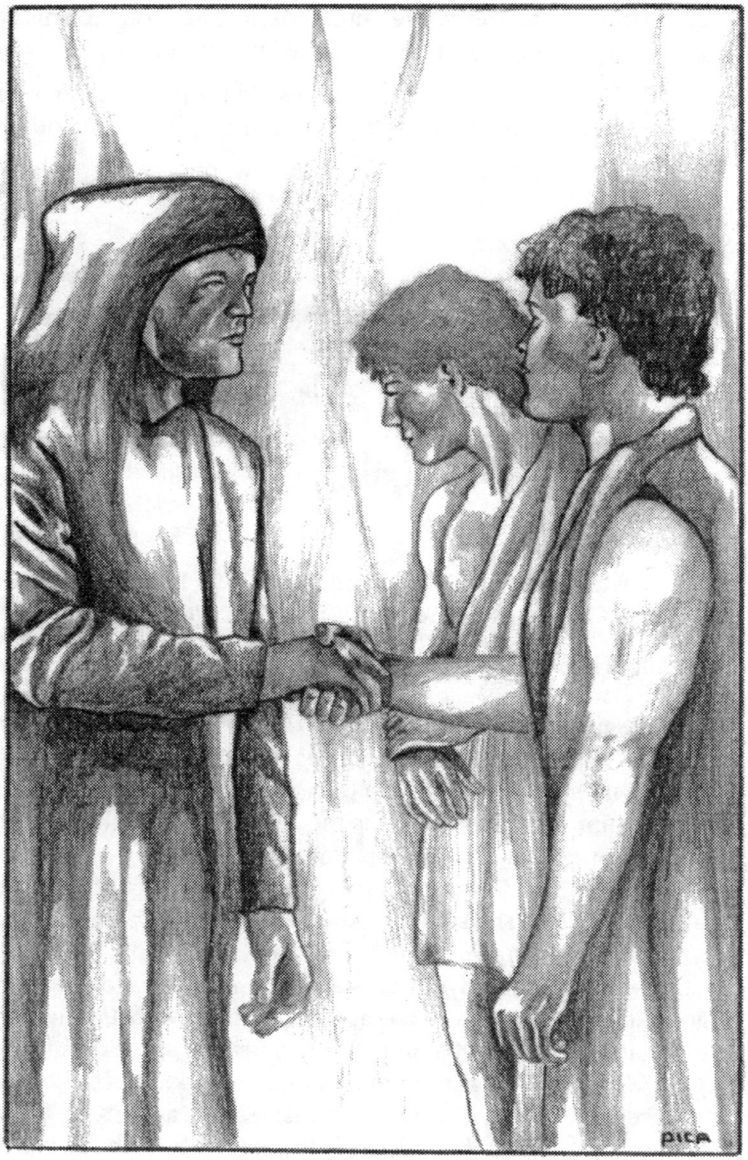
PICA

Canto IV

Virgil and Dante see four shadows: Homer (ancient Greek poet and author of *The Iliad* and *The Odyssey*), Horace (ancient Latin poet who lived in Rome), Ovid (ancient Roman poet who wrote of creation until the time of Caesar), and Lucan (ancient Roman poet who wrote of Caesar). The two pay honor to Virgil and ask Dante to join their ranks. Dante also sees Electra (daughter of Atlas and mother of Dardanus, the founder of Troy), Caesar (dictator of Rome 100–44 B.C.), Camilla (maiden-warrior dedicated to the service of Diana, the goddess of the hunt), Penthesilea (queen of the Amazons and killed by Achilles), Latinus (king of Latium where Aeneas lands), Lavinia (daughter of Latinus and wife of Aeneas), Brutus (aroused the Romans to overthrow Tarquinius Superbus, who had a son that had angered Lucretia), Marcia (Cato's wife, who was given to a friend, and returned to Cato of Utica), Cornelia (wife of Tiberius Sempronius Gracchus and mother of two famous Tribunes; celebrated by people of Rome), Julia (daughter of Julius Caesar), Lucrece (woman outraged by son of Tarquinius Superbus), Saladin (Sultan of Egypt, model of chivalry, and hero of the Third Crusade in the twelfth century), Aristotle (the master of the men who know), Socrates (philosopher of Athens), Plato (philosopher of Athens and student of Socrates), Diogenes (Greek philosopher), Thales (Ionic philosopher and one of the seven wise men of Greece), Zeno (Greek philosopher), Democritus (philosopher), Empedocles (Greek philosopher who established idea of four elements—earth, water, air, fire), Anaxagoras (Ionic philosopher), Heraclitus (Greek philosopher), Dioscorides (Greek physician), Tully (Roman orator and author), Orpheus (one of Jason's Argonauts and mythical Greek poet), Linus (mythical poet of Greece), Seneca (a moralist, tutor to Nero, and Roman philosopher), Euclid (mathematician who lived in Alexandria), Ptolemy (mathematician, geographer, and astronomer at Alexandria), Galen (Greek physician), Hippocrates (physician on the island of Cos and author of the Hippocratic oath), Avicen (Arabian physician), Averrhoes (a Spanish Moor who lived in the twelfth century, scholar and philosopher, translator of Aristotle), and others.

Eventually the original band of six—Homer, Horace, Ovid, Lucan, Virgil, and Dante—dwindles to Virgil and Dante. The descent to Hell begins.

Analysis

Dante knows not how he got to the edges of the pit of Hell; earlier he knew not how he got to the woods. Dante is, evidently, still lost and must count on others for guidance. Recognition of this dependence on God is necessary for salvation so the helplessness is significant.

The paleness of Virgil is a contrast to the black pit of Hell; the blackness of Hell symbolizes the sin contained within. From the pit comes the sounds of those in anguish; these sounds are as much a shock to Dante as are the sights he sees.

When Dante asks if anyone has ever left this First Circle, Virgil tells him that one with a crown (Jesus) came and freed some; it is significant that while Virgil and Dante are in the pit, the name of Jesus is not spoken aloud.

Study Questions

1. Where is Dante when he awakes from his swoon?
2. What causes Dante to wake from his swoon?
3. What causes the thunder Dante heard?
4. What is the sound of the first circumference?
5. Who is in the First Circle?
6. Who are the four mighty shades?
7. Dante says that the group of six dwindles to two. What does he mean?
8. What is the occupation of the "men that know"?
9. Why is the first circle called "Limbo"?
10. Who is the first father that the one with crowns took from the First Circle?

Canto V

Answers

1. Dante is on the brink of the pit when he awakes.
2. Thunder wakes Dante from his swoon.
3. The thunder that Dante hears is the sound of the wails of anguish from the pit.
4. The sound of the first circumference is that of sighing.
5. In the First Circle are those who are blameless but are unbaptized and lived before the days of Christendom.
6. Homer, Horace, Ovid and Lucan are the four shadows.
7. Horace, Homer, Ovid, and Lucan stay behind and Virgil and Dante move forward.
8. The men that know are philosophers and teachers.
9. The First Circle is called Limbo because the souls there are neither in Heaven nor in Hell.
10. The first father whom the one with crowns rescued was Adam.

Suggested Essay Topics

1. What are the indications that you have seen that Dante is lost?
2. Research one of those whom Dante sees about him in the First Circle. Write a paper about that person. In conclusion, express why you think that person is in the First Circle and not further down in the pit

Canto V

New Characters:

Minos: *Legendary King of Crete who occupies the threshold of the Second Circle and assigns places to the damned*

Those Guilty of the Sin of Lust: *Include Lancelot, Cleopatra, Achilles*

Francesca and Paolo: *Adulterous couple killed by Francesca's husband, Gianciotto da Verruchio*

Summary

As Dante descends from the First Circle, he finds that the Second Circle holds greater woe. As he goes further down into Hell, he finds those guilty of the sin of lust. The threshold to the Second Circle is guarded by Minos; each person who enters must confess to Minos, who decides their fate. The place is dark and the sounds of the souls reach the ears of Dante.

Dante sees first the mistress of Babel. Next he notes Cleopatra and Helen in the Second Circle; both had experienced lust and yielded to their desires. Men, too, had yielded to lust and now reside in the Second Circle. From his studies of history and mythology Dante recognizes three: Achilles, Paris, and Tristram.

Dante speaks with Francesca (wife of Gianciotto da Verruchio and lover to his brother Paolo). She tells Dante of how she and Paolo had been reading of Sir Lancelot, Guinevere, and Galleot and of how she died at the hand of her husband when he found that she was unfaithful. Dante sympathizes with Paolo and Francesca and swoons in pity.

Analysis

The further one descends into Hell, the greater the sins represented and the greater their punishment. Whereas those in the First Circle merely sigh, those in the Second Circle are crying out with woe. Minos, a legendary judge of the underworld, hears the confessions, but he does not forgive the sin; rather he decides which area one must go to in order to receive the deserved punishment for the sin.

The Second Circle is the place in which carnal sinners reside. It is the first punishment area for sins of incontinence. Those who do not exercise will power go here; the sins they commit are sins of lust, or sins of the flesh. These carnal sinners are thrust about forever by winds.

Among the souls, Virgil notes "the mistress of Babylon." "Babylon" could refer to the ancient city of Babylon in Asia Minor

Canto V

or to the great tower where Scripture says that many languages began. (The construction of the tower was a result of a desire for or a lust for power.)

Two famous women are residents of the Second Circle: Cleopatra (the Egyptian queen and lover of Antony and Julius Caesar) and Helen (wife of King Menelaus of Sparta and prisoner of Paris of Troy). The men include Achilles (Greek warrior killed by the Trojans by promising him the hand of a Trojan woman if he would join their cause), Paris (Trojan captor of Helen), and Tristram (lover of the wife of King Mark of Cornwall and killed by King Mark upon his discovery).

Francesca talks of how she and Paolo had read of the love of Sir Lancelot and Guinevere. The book they read tells of Galleot who serves as a go-between for Lancelot and the Queen. Like the characters in the book, Francesca and Guinevere yielded to sins of lust.

The punishment of sins of the flesh is to continue to experience the sin; the sinners drift in the wind and remember the love. Because of the choices which they made, the lustful will never experience redemption and peace.

Study Questions

1. Why does Francesca's heart still hurt and ache?
2. How does Dante react to Francesca's tale?
3. What does Francesca say is the greatest sadness in this place?
4. What is the punishment in this Second Circle?
5. What caused Francesca to commit the sin of lust with Paolo?
6. How did Francesca die?
7. Why does Dante not tell the reader of the trip from Circle One to Circle Two and from Circle Two to Circle Three?
8. What does Minos do?
9. In Canto III and in Canto V Dante refers to will and power being one. Where is this place where will and power are one?
10. What does it mean when Dante says that he is grieved by the way in which the murder of Francesca and Paolo came about?

Answers

1. Francesca's husband murdered her without her having a chance to repent; she will be punished eternally. She will continue to remember the love.
2. Dante cries and swoons with pity at Francesca's tale.
3. The greatest sadness is to remember the happy times.
4. The punishment in the Second Circle is to drift in the wind and to continue to remember the sin; there is no peace or redemption.
5. Francesca and Paolo were reading of Sir Lancelot and Guinevere when they, too, yielded to sin.
6. Francesca and Paolo were murdered by Francesca's husband Gianciotto da Verruchio when he found them.
7. Dante swoons when he makes the trip from Circle One to Circle Two and when he makes the trip from Circle Two to Circle Three.
8. Minos admits people to Hell. He listens to their confessions and then assigns a place in Hell to them.
9. Will and power are one in Heaven.
10. The "way in which it all came about" is a quotation from *The Inferno* which may refer to the way in which Gianciotto da Verruchio killed Paolo and Francesca. It may also be a reference to the fact that they were killed without a chance to confess their sins and seek forgiveness.

Suggested Essay Topics

1. Explain how the sins themselves are punishment in Hell. Use the First and Second Circles as examples.
2. Compare and contrast Minos with Christ.

Canto VI

New Characters:

Cerberus: *Three-headed dog who watches over the Third Circle of Hell*

The Inhabitants of Circle Three: *The gluttonous*

Ciacco: *Gluttonous male inhabitant of Florence; nickname means "pig"*

Summary

In Circle Three Dante finds constant rain, sleet, snow, and hail. Cerberus, the three-headed dog, meets Dante and Virgil; Virgil manages to quiet the dog's attacks by throwing mud from the ground into the three mouths. All around Virgil and Dante are gluttons lying in the mud.

One of the gluttons named Ciacco is from Florence. He speaks to Dante and Virgil. Ciacco predicts that the political strife between the Black and White factions in Florence will continue and bloodshed will come. The Wood party will drive out the other faction but within three suns, he tells them, the confidence of the Woods will suffer a fall. The other faction will rise after this time.

Ciacco answers Dante's questions about the location of the worthy men Tegghiaio and Farinata; the zealous Rusticucci; Mosca and Arrigo; "and the rest as well." Ciacco tells Dante that they are all deeper in Hell.

As a last request, Ciacco asks Dante to recall his name once Dante reaches the world again.

Virgil tells Dante that more woe is to come. They continue their descent and find the great enemy Pluto ahead.

Analysis

The constant rain, sleet, snow, and hail create mud; this mud is the steady diet of the gluttons who had overindulged in their earthly life. The three-headed dog is a fitting guard for Circle Three because the monster is uncouth and difficult to satisfy, like the gluttons.

The Divine Comedy I: Inferno

Canto VI

Ciacco tells Dante that each of the five men from Florence is further down in Hell. Tegghiaio (Tegghiaio Aldobrandi; a resident of Florence, a spokesperson of the Guelph nobles, and an advisor against the Siena attack that resulted in the defeat of the Florentines), Arrigo (a Florentine Ghibelline), Mosca (Mosca dei Lamberti; a noble in Florence), Rusticucci (Jacopo Rusticucci; a wealthy statesman of humble origin; whose evil-tempered wife drives him into vice), and Farinata (Farinata Degli Uberti; resident of Florence and a Ghibelline leader) are the five men from Florence. Ciacco tells Dante that the five are further down in Hell. This means that the five are guilty of more serious sins.

The further into Hell that Virgil and Dante travel, the more anguish they experience.

Study Questions

1. What is the atmosphere like in Circle Three?
2. Of what crimes were the souls in Circle Three guilty?
3. From where did the gluttonous soul who talks to Dante and Virgil in Circle Three come?
4. From what city did Dante come?
5. What are the three sparks from Hell sowed in every person's breast?
6. Who is the great enemy that Dante and Virgil will find at the next descent?
7. What does the word Ciacco mean?
8. Who is the guardian of Circle Three?
9. What were the gluttons eating in Hell?
10. What is the "Enemy Power?"

Answers

1. The atmosphere in Circle Three includes rain, sleet, snow, and hail.
2. The souls in Circle Three are guilty of gluttony.

3. The gluttonous soul who spoke with Dante and Virgil was from Florence.
4. Dante was from Florence.
5. The three sparks were Avarice, Envy, and Pride.
6. Pluto will be at the next level down.
7. The word Ciacco means "pig."
8. The three-headed dog Cerberus was the guardian of Circle Three.
9. The gluttons were eating mud in Hell.
10. The "Enemy Power" is a reference to Christ, the enemy of sin.

Suggested Essay Topics
1. Compare and contrast Circle Two with Circle Three.
2. What did Ciacco mean when he said that Hell had put three sparks in human breasts?
3. Why did Ciacco want Dante to speak his name on earth? Explain your answer.

Canto VII

New Characters:

Pluto: *God of the underworld and riches; at entrance to the Fourth Circle*

The Hoarders and the Spendthrifts: *Condemned to push and pull great weights for their sins*

The Wrathful: *Those who are ferocious and those who withdraw in black sulkiness and can find no joy; condemned to a marsh*

Summary

As Dante and Virgil enter the Fourth Circle, they encounter Pluto. Pluto begins to say a chant to Satan. Virgil reminds Dante that Satan has no power over them.

Canto VII

Dante compares the movements of the souls in the Fourth Circle with the waves caused by the *Charybdis*. The souls hoarded and squandered in their life and for punishment they must move great weights with their chests. Those who squandered are pushing the weights away; those who hoarded are pushing the weights toward themselves. The pushing and pulling results in bumping and bruising. Virgil explains that Luck, through Divine Providence, is responsible for the distribution of wealth; riches do not remain in one nation or with one family for long because of the workings of Luck.

Virgil and Dante cross near a bubbling spring which had cut a cleft in the rock; the pair go down a stair into a marsh—the Styx, one of the most famous features of classical Hell. In the mire beneath, Dante sees people fighting and tearing one another with their teeth; these are the people who expressed their wrath openly or actively. The passively wrathful are those who lie sighing beneath the mire of the marsh; they had taken no pleasure in life and instead had retreated into a black mood or sullenness.

At the end of their path, Dante and Virgil see a tall tower.

Analysis

Dante and Virgil hear the chant uttered by Pluto. Though the exact meaning is not clear, it seems that Pluto is calling on Satan for help. Satan would be Pluto's only source of help since Pluto consciously made a choice against God.

The way to deeper sin and punishment is becoming more clear to Dante. The initial slip to sin and punishment is barely noticed. Dante, for instance, did not notice the move from Circle One to Circle Two or from Circle Two to Circle Three; he did not notice when he originally became lost. Now, however, the way is becoming more evident as sin becomes more deliberate.

In *The Odyssey* the *Charybdis* is a sea monster; three times a day this monster sucks down the sea water and spits it out again. The resulting waves pound nearby ships.

Those who squandered in life are pushing the weights away as eternal punishment. Those who hoarded in life are pulling the weights toward themselves. The pushing and pulling results in the shades bumping and bruising one another; this physical conflict is symbolic of the philosophic conflict that is evident between the two groups. The actively wrathful continue to make contact with one another in Hell; the passively wrathful withdraw in Hell to the mud just as they once withdrew from the mainstream in life.

Dante believes that avarice is the fault of the clergy; therefore, clerics largely compose the population of this level. On line 39 Dante asks, "...were they each a clerk?"

Study Questions
1. Who guards the Fourth Circle?
2. What sins have been committed by those in the Fourth Circle?
3. Describe how the squanderers and the hoarders are punished.
4. What is the name of the marsh in the Fourth Circle?
5. Where are the passively wrathful in the Fourth Circle?
6. How does Dante travel within the Fourth Circle?
7. The Fourth Circle is the last of the circles of Incontinence. What is "incontinence"?
8. What did Virgil and Dante find at the foot of the path and stairs?
9. To whom do nations owe the credit for the amassing great wealth or the blame for not amassing this wealth?
10. Why did Virgil encourage Dante to move more rapidly?

Answers
1. Pluto guards the Fourth Circle.
2. The souls in the Fourth Circle are guilty of squandering, hoarding, and wrath.
3. The squanderers and the hoarders are being punished by being forced to push and pull weights with their chests.
4. The name of the marsh is the Styx.
5. The passively wrathful are underneath the mire of the marsh.

6. Dante travels by a path and down stairs.
7. "Incontinence" refers to sins of self-indulgence; these sins imply a lack of will and are sins against the self.
8. Virgil and Dante found a tall tower at the foot of the path and the stairs.
9. Nations should blame or praise Luck for their amassing or not amassing great wealth.
10. Virgil encouraged Dante to move more swiftly since the stars that were there when they began their journey were no longer visible and the High Powers had not authorized a long stay.

Suggested Essay Topics

1. Compare and contrast the use of mud and mire in the punishment of the gluttons and the use of mud and mire in the punishment of the actively and passively wrathful.
2. Pluto is a god of riches. Explain his presence at the entrance to the Fourth Circle.
3. Compare and contrast the Styx and the Acheron.

Canto VIII

New Characters:

Phlegyas: *The mariner on the Styx who comes for Dante and Virgil*

Filippo Argenti: *Florentine resident; had differed politically with Dante*

Summary

At the top of the tower Dante and Virgil see two sparks of light; in the distance two sparks answer and Phlegyas, the angry oarsman, arrives. Phlegyas does not like the fact that Dante and Virgil are only visitors and not to be permanent residents of the area.

Dante expresses anger toward the soul in the mud who tries to hold their boat. Dante expresses this contempt toward the

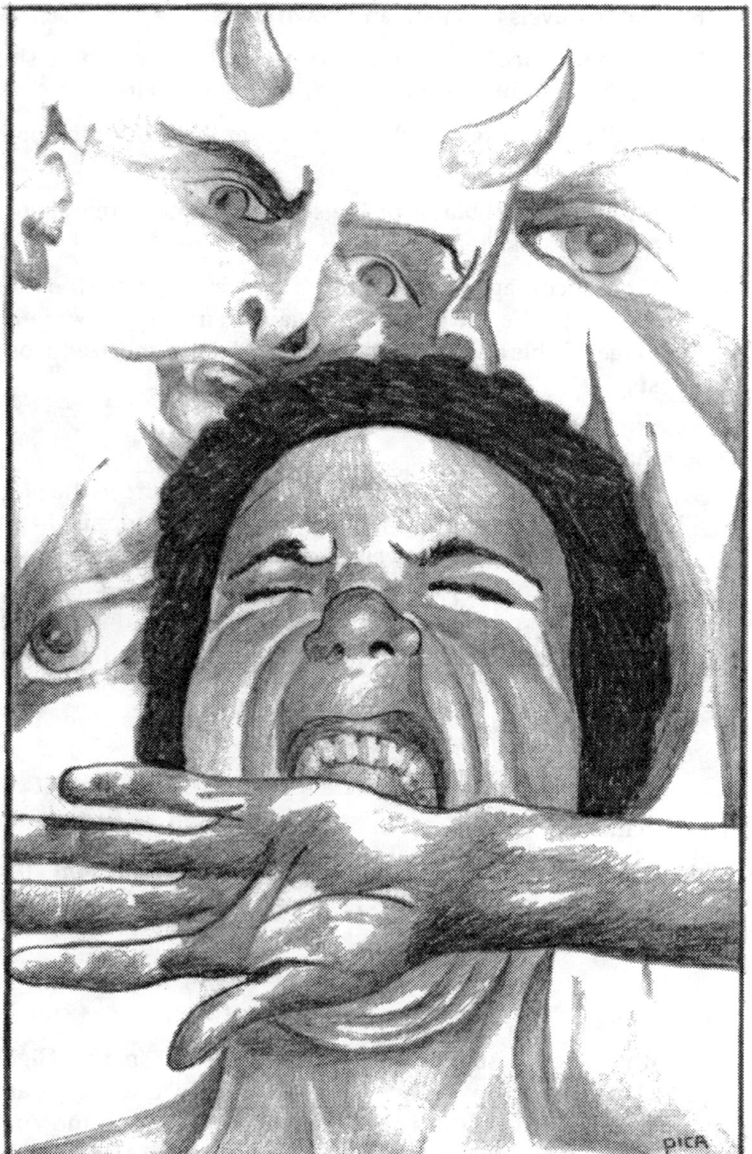
PICA

Canto VIII

man—whom he recognizes. Virgil commends Dante for his expression of contempt toward the shade and agrees with Dante's actions. Virgil goes to the gates of the City of Dis, or Lower Hell. In the lower regions, more serious sins find greater punishment. The enemy, however, slams the gate in Virgil's face. When Virgil is unable to enter, he calls to ask for help.

Analysis

The ferryman Phlegyas may be the same mythological Greek King who burned Apollo's temple upon finding that Apollo was in love with his daughter. Apollo killed Phlegyas and condemned Phlegyas to Hades. Because of his own wrathful and sacrilegious actions, Phlegyas would be an appropriate oarsman between the Wrathful and Impious Souls.

There are several possible explanations for Dante's anger toward the soul in the mud. First, since the wrathful had accepted cruelty and denied pity in life, in death no pity could be given them. Another reason for the unkind remarks might be that Dante is beginning to change and to reject sin. A third, obvious reason might be the fact that the remarks and actions of the wrathful soul in the mud caused anger in Dante. A fourth reason might be that the soul in the mud was an enemy of Dante when they were both in Florence; in fact Dante states that he knows the person. Some interpreters believe the soul to be Filippo Argenti.

The reader should note that Dante's actions in Canto VIII vary from the tears that Dante originally shed when he first saw the shades in Hell. Virgil's support of Dante's anger is because Virgil, as a man of reason, is bitter toward those who would deliberately choose sin.

Virgil's having to ask for help in order to gain admission to the City of Dis symbolizes that people cannot make this trip alone but must have permission from a higher power to continue onto the area of greater sins. The fact that Virgil has difficulty gaining admission is an indication that Virgil has not committed those sins which would gain him entrance to the lower parts of Hell.

Study Questions
1. Who rows the boat for Dante and Virgil?
2. What is the signal used to send for the oarsman?
3. What does the soul in the mud mean when he asks who is here before his time?
4. Why is the oarsman angry when he sees who has come for a ride?
5. What is the name of the soul in the mud who causes Dante to show anger?
6. What is Dante's reaction to the pulling and hauling that Filippo Argenti receives?
7. Dante says at one point that his gentle father has left him. To whom is he referring?
8. What is the name of the city at which they arrive?
9. How is Virgil received at the gates of the City of Dis?
10. What does Virgil have to do to gain admittance?

Answers
1. Phlegyas rows the boat for Dante and Virgil.
2. The signal that is used to send for the oarsman is two signal lights in the tower.
3. The soul in the mud wants to know who is here in Hell before his death.
4. The oarsman is angry when he sees who has come for a ride because they are not going to be permanent residents of Hell at this time.
5. The soul in the mud is Filippo Argenti, a resident of Florence.
6. Dante thanks and praises God for the pulling and hauling that Filippo Argenti receives from the souls in Hell.

Canto IX

7. Dante is referring to Virgil when he says that his father has left him.
8. The city is named Dis, or the city named after the King of Hell. Dante refers to this king as Satan.
9. Virgil is turned away from the City of Dis.
10. Virgil has to ask for help in order to gain admittance to Dis.

Suggested Essay Topics
1. What does it mean when Dante says that the boat does not seem to carry a load at all until Dante entered? Explain your answer.
2. Why do you think that Dante shows anger toward the soul in the mud?

Canto IX

New Characters:

Three Furies: *Queen Medusa's handmaids: Alecto, Magaera, Tisiphone*

The Heavenly Messenger: *Helper to Virgil and Dante; possibly St. Paul*

The Heretics: *In open graves; had trusted reason rather than the church*

Medusa: *Evil, serpent-haired goddess; could turn people to stone*

Summary

Dante begins to lose hope when Virgil is denied entrance to the City of Dis. Even Virgil is pale at this point. Dante asks Virgil if he has ever made the trip before and Virgil tells him that he had once gone to the City of Dis at the insistence of a witch named Erichtho. Virgil's task at that time had been to bring a soul from Judas's circle in the lower realms. Dante, however, does not listen

The Divine Comedy I: Inferno

Canto IX

well because he is watching the red-hot battlements (breastworks) of the tower.

Dante's eyes are drawn upward to the tower, where he sees three shapes: the three Furies named Alecto, Magaera, and Tisiphone. They threaten to summon Medusa to turn Dante and Virgil to stone. Virgil turns Dante around to prevent his looking in case Medusa does come.

A great wind blows and then one comes from Heaven to help the two travelers. The messenger chastises the spirits and reminds them how Cerberus had tried to rebel, was chastised, and still bears the scars from the experience.

The heavenly messenger returns to other matters, and Virgil and Dante continue. They see that the stone slabs designed to cover the graves in this area are no longer in place; the souls within the open tombs sigh aloud. Flames leap forth from the graves.

Analysis

Dante is quick to lose his faith when Virgil cannot gain quick admission into the City of Dis. Virgil himself says that help is a long time in coming; this could be a reference to the delay in the second coming of Christ or an allusion to the fact that people in dire straits should seek help quickly since they cannot survive on their own.

Some interpreters see Dante's question about Virgil's previous journey as a ploy to take Virgil's mind from the pressures of the moment. Other references suggest that Dante is seeking to rebuild Virgil's confidence by reminding him that he has successfully made the trip once.

Erichtho is a witch with power over the dead. Virgil says that he made a trip at another time to bring a shade up from the lower realms for her. Since Dante does not listen carefully to the explanation that Virgil gives for removing the shade from the lower realms, the reader (and most interpreters of *The Inferno*) are at a loss as to Virgil's explanation beyond the fact that he was bringing up one from Judas's circle. (Supposedly this particular Judas is Judas Iscariot, who betrayed Jesus.)

Dante refers to the Furies also by their Greek name of Erinyes. The three Furies worry and fret those who have committed sins and have a guilty conscience. The three Furies threaten to fetch

Medusa, with her hair of serpents. A person has only to look at Medusa to be turned to stone; for this reason, Virgil asks Dante to turn away. The reference to stone may symbolize the hardening of one's heart, a conscious act which prevents a sinner from gaining forgiveness. The Furies are like the guilty conscience of a sinner and Medusa is like the hardening heart of a sinner; just as the Furies and Medusa keep Virgil and Dante from entering Hell, a guilty conscience and a hard heart keep sinners from entering Heaven.

At this point a messenger from Heaven arrives. This messenger asks the spirits why they kick against the pricks of the great Will. It is possible that this messenger, who chastises the Furies, is the Apostle Paul. It was Paul who heard, on his way to Damascus, a heavenly voice asking him why he kicked against the pricks; most interpreters consider this question to be an inquiry as to why Paul (or the spirits) persecuted Christ. Again, Christ is not called by name in this wicked place; rather the spirits refer to "the great Will."

The travelers hear the sighing of the heretics within their open graves and see the flames shooting from the open tombs. The tombs have iron outside and flames within; the flames may symbolize punishment and the iron may symbolize the iron will which brought sinners here. Iron is impenetrable; thus, sinners are bound to the suffering caused by their own sins.

Study Questions
1. From where did Virgil hope to get help?
2. Who is Erichtho?
3. Why had Virgil been in Hell before?
4. Who are the Furies?
5. Who was the queen whom the three goddesses served?
6. Describe Medusa.
7. What are the tombs like near the City of Dis?
8. How does the heavenly messenger open the gate?
9. Why do you think the heavenly messenger spent so little time with Dante and Virgil?
10. Who are the heretics?

Canto IX 45

Answers

1. Virgil hopes to get help from Heaven.
2. Erichtho is a witch.
3. Virgil had been in Hell previously to fetch a spirit from Judas's circle.
4. The Furies are three goddesses who haunt those who commit certain crimes.
5. The queen is Medusa.
6. Medusa is a queen with serpents for hair; she could turn people to stone if they looked on her.
7. The slabs on the graves have been pushed aside; the fire and souls within can be seen and heard.
8. The heavenly messenger waves a wand over the gate and it opens.
9. The heavenly messenger does not spend much time with Dante and Virgil because he had other duties and because he dislikes Hell.
10. The heretics are those who lie within the open graves and who in life had trusted their reason rather than the Church.

Suggested Essay Topics

1. Virgil says that the witch Erichtho wanted to "call back the shades to their dead clay." What do you think he meant by that? Please explain fully.
2. Describe the souls in punishment in the Nether Hell, the City of Dis. Why are they there? What is their punishment?

Canto X

New Characters:

Farinata degli Uberti: *Leader of the Ghibellines, the party responsible for killing Dante's grandfather; favored imperial authority*

Canto X

Cavalcante dei Cavalcanti: *A shade who was once of the Guelph party*

Summary

Virgil and Dante pass near the city walls. Virgil reminds Dante that in the days of Jehoshaphat those buried shall come anew. They are greeted by Farinata degli Uberti. Dante and Farinata exchange words about the fighting between the Ghibellines and the Guelph parties through the years. Farinata foretells the length of Dante's exile and explains that the dead have knowledge of the future. Farinata refers to the queen which rules the lower regions when he talks with Dante. He makes reference to the queen of the Nether Hell.

Another spirit—that of Cavalcante of the Guelph party—appears and asks about his son Guido dei Cavalcanti, who was Dante's best friend and a fellow poet. Dante becomes aware that the spirits can see and prophesy the future but that they have difficulty seeing things as they are now. Dante accidentally reveals to Cavalcante that his son is dead.

After Dante finds out the identity of some of those who lie in the graveyard, the shade tells Dante that when he sees one whose eyes are able to see all things (Beatrice), he will learn the meaning of life.

Analysis

Farinata was an enemy of Dante in life. The two had been enemies through the years because of differing political beliefs. They compare stories of victories and defeats in the past wars. They discuss a rout of Guelphs in 1248, a return in 1251, a rout in 1260, and a return in 1266, which made it impossible for the Ghibellines to return to power.

Cavalcante dei Cavalcanti is the shade who is devastated to find that his son (Guido) is dead. Since Cavalcante is an Epicurean who does not believe in life after death, he is devastated.

Thousand of heretics who trusted their own knowledge over that of the Church lie in the graveyard. The shade Farinata tells that these sinners include Emperor Frederick II and the Cardinal Ottaviano degli Ubaldini (1210-73), a violent Ghibelline.

Several references in Canto X need explanation. The shade Farinata tells Dante that he will know the full meaning of life when he stands before one whose eyes see all that is complete; this is a reference to Beatrice. Two references in Canto X are to Jehoshaphat, a valley which will be the scene of the last judgment. The queen who reigns below is Proserpine, the Earth-Mother whom Pluto stole and carried to Dis.

Study Questions

1. Dante addresses the power that "wheels" him. To whom is he referring?
2. What is an Epicurean?
3. Who is the family enemy that Dante encounters in the graveyard?
4. One of the shades inquires of a family member to Dante. About whom does he ask?
5. What does he find out about this family member?
6. With whom does the shade say he is lying in that graveyard?
7. Name the term used to refer to Christ in Canto X?
8. About what do Dante and Farinata argue in Canto X?
9. What is the reference to Beatrice in Canto X?
10. Who is the queen who reigns below?

Answers

1. Dante is referring to Virgil.
2. An Epicurean is one who believes that when the body dies the soul dies also.
3. The family enemy that Dante finds in the graveyard is Farinata.
4. The shade asked about his son.
5. When Dante accidentally uses the word *felt*, he reveals that the shade's son (Guido) is dead.

Canto XI

6. The shade says that he is lying with thousands, including Frederick II and the Cardinal Ottaviano degli Ubaldini.
7. In Canto X Christ is called the All-Guider.
8. Dante and Farinata argue about the battles fought between their two political parties.
9. The reference to Beatrice is made at the end of Canto X when the shade Farinata tells Dante that he will know the truth about life when he stands before one whose eyes know all things complete.
10. The queen who reigns below is Proserpine, the Earth-Mother whom Pluto captured and carried away to Hades.

Suggested Essay Topics

1. What is the shade's response when Dante asks him with whom he lies?
2. When does the shade say that Dante will learn the meaning of life? What do you think he means by that?

Canto XI

Summary

As the two poets pause before entering the Seventh Circle, they note the writing on a vault by which they rest. The writing indicates that the vault holds Pope Anastasius whom Photinus lured. As they wait, Dante asks that they spend their time well.

Virgil complies; he explains that the three circles below them are devoted to sins of violence. The acts of violence committed by souls in these circles are directed against God, against self, and against neighbor. Since God hates sins against neighbors the most, this circle is most distant from God and closer to the bottom of the pit. Virgil explains also that there are two kinds of fraud: that which betrays the confidence of humanity in general and that which betrays the confidence of a particular person. The second type of fraud becomes even more treacherous. Furthermore, the poet tells Virgil why there are levels of Hell and the punishment for each.

Virgil goes into great detail as to why usury is a sin and why contempt of art or Nature is contempt of God. Virgil uses many terms connected with the stars to remind Dante that the time to resume their journey has come. At the end of Canto XI the guide leads and Dante again follows.

Analysis

Overcome by the stench of the pit, Virgil and Dante pause. The inscription they read on the vault indicates that Photinus lured the Pope inside into sin. Photinus was a deacon from Thessalonica whom the Pope gave communion even though Photinus was a member of the Church of Constantinople.

Virgil informs Dante that the next three circles are arranged according to whom they offended: God, self, or neighbor. Sins against one's neighbor are closest to the bottom of the pit. Using Aristotle's *Ethics* to provide examples, Virgil also explains why there are levels of Hell. Murderers, robbers, and plunderers are in ring one; those who rob themselves of your world, who gamble and waste their purse are in ring two; those who dishonor God's name and who commit the sins of Sodom (homosexuality) and Cahors (usury) are in ring three. The poet reminds Dante that people, after Genesis, ought to get their own bread and make prosperity for all. Those who engage in usury, or money lending, scorn Nature, the followers of Nature (Art), and God because they refuse to use the means of survival given to them by God.

Virgil reminds Dante that the Wain (Ursa Major) was over the Caurus (northwest wind) and that the time was that of the Fishes, or Pisces (mid-February to mid-March); this means that the time is two hours before sunrise (probably 4 a.m.) on Holy Saturday. Some interpreters point out that Virgil probably could not see the sky from Hell.

Study Questions

1. What sin does Virgil say that people—but not animals—are subject to commit and that God hates worst?
2. In which ring would one find murderers, people who are violent with their hands, and robbers?

Canto XI

3. In which ring would one find those who gamble, waste their money, and rob themselves of goods?
4. What is the sin of Sodom?
5. What is the sin of Cahors?
6. Where would one find flatterers, sorcerers, hypocrites, and cheats?
7. Which is least blameworthy: incontinence, vice, or brute bestiality?
8. What does Dante say will heal all light which was dim?
9. Contempt of art and contempt of Nature are the same, according to Dante, in that they express contempt of whom?
10. What does Dante define as a breach of trust against the confiding?

Answers

1. People are subject to commit the sin of fraud but animals cannot. God hates the sin of fraud more than any other sin.
2. In the first ring one would find murders, people who are violent with their hands, and robbers
3. In ring two one would find those who gamble, waste their money, and rob themselves of goods.
4. The sin of Sodom is homosexuality.
5. The sin of Cahors is usury.
6. Flatterers, sorcerers, hypocrites, and cheats are in the second ring.
7. The sin of incontinence is least blameworthy.
8. Dante says sunlight will heal all light which is dim.
9. Contempt of art and contempt of Nature are the same, according to Dante, as they show contempt of God.

10. Dante defines fraud as a breach of trust against the confiding.

Suggested Essay Topics
1. Dante describes three circles containing souls who have committed sins worse than others. Which sins are more severe? Why?
2. Why is usury a sin? Explain in detail.

Canto XII

New Characters:

Minotaur: *Creature with the head of a bull and the body of a man*

Centaurs: *Creatures with the heads of men and the bodies of horses*

Chiron: *Chief centaur*

Deianira: *Wife of Hercules; dipped his shirt in blood of Nessus*

Nessus: *Centaur who tried to carry off Deianira (wife of Hercules); his blood on Hercules's shirt caused Hercules so much pain that Hercules burned himself to death*

Violent Sinners: *Guilty of violence, included Pyrrhus, Achilles' cruel son*

Summary
Dante and Virgil see a place where a great landslide has occurred and where the Minotaur has come forth from the resulting cleft. Virgil comments that when he passed that way before the rock had not yet fallen; he states that the great Prince had entered and taken His prey from Dis.

Dante and Virgil look down in the valley and see the river of blood; this boiling river (the Phlegethon) is used to punish those who were violent in life. On the bank at the side of the river, Dante sees centaurs racing through the woods with bows and quivers; their arrows keep the violent from escaping from the river of boil-

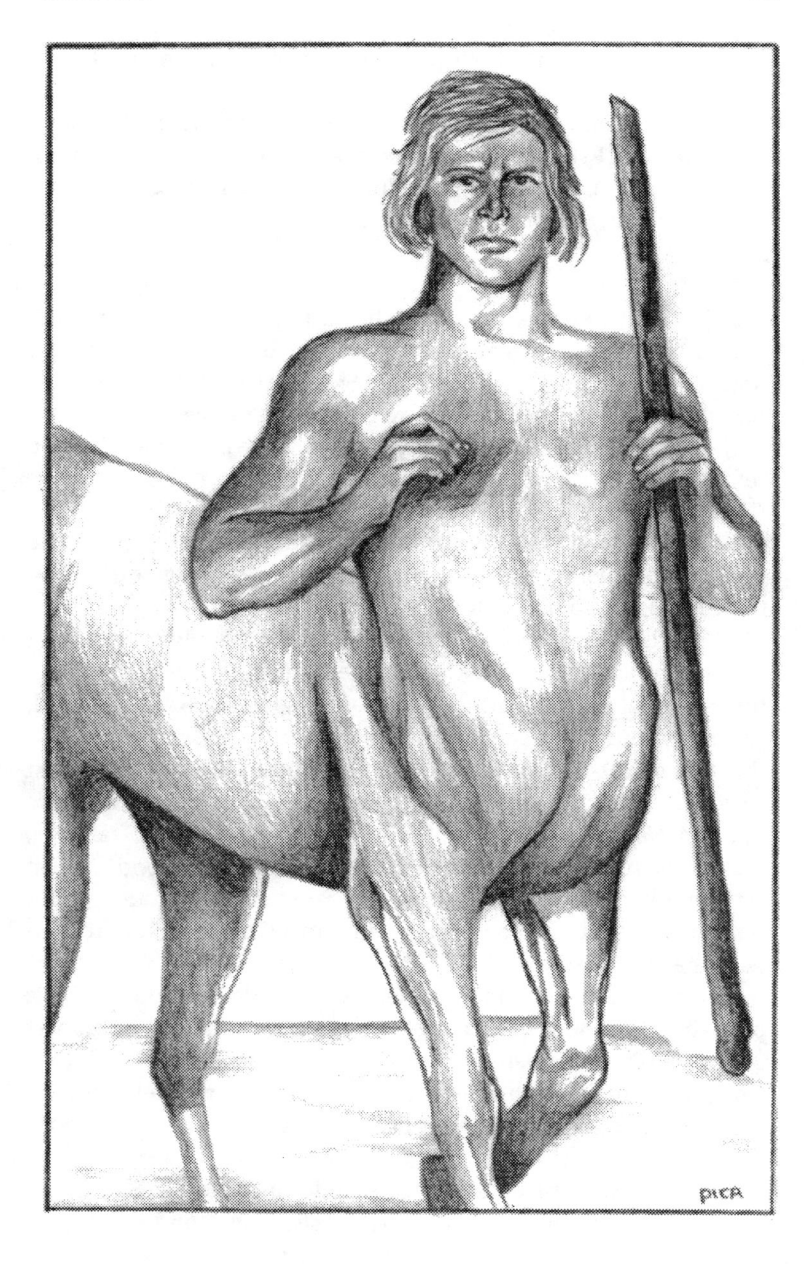

Canto XII

ing blood. This canto includes some specific persons: Chiron, Deianira, Nessus, and Pholus.

The travelers see the tyrants Alexander, Dionysius, Azzolino, and Obizzo d' Este. The centaur points out Pyrrhus, Sextus, Attila, and the Pazzian and Cornetan Riniers; he turns, crosses the ford again, and leaves Dante and Virgil alone.

Analysis

The landslide was a result of the earthquake at Christ's crucifixion. The Minotaur is a monster with the head of a bull and the body of a man and is guardian of the Seventh Circle. "The rock that had not fallen" has two meanings: Christ had not yet died and the rock with the Minotaur had not yet fallen. "The prey from Dis" is a reference to those whom Christ had rescued from the pit; Canto IV discusses this rescue.

The boiling river of blood is a fitting punishment for those who in life used violence against their neighbor. They had caused blood to be shed; blood now punishes them.

Several specific characters in this Canto probably need further explanation. Virgil and Dante see centaurs—half man and half horse—regulating the punishment of those in the River of Blood. Chiron is chief centaur. Chiron tells Nessus to guide Dante across the shallowest part of the stream and Virgil tells Dante to trust Nessus's authority; the centaur knows better than Virgil in these matters. Nessus, who attempted to steal Hercules' wife Deianira, died at the hand of Hercules; Deianira used Nessus' blood as a dip for Hercules' shirt. The blood was so caustic that Hercules could not stand the pain; Hercules burned himself to death rather than bear the torture of the blood.

The tyrants whom the travelers see include Alexander, who is probably Alexander the Great; Dionysius, who may be either the Sicilian father or son since both were tyrants of Sicily; Azzolino, a Ghibelline; and Obizzo d' Este, a thirteenth century Guelph nobleman who had a reputation for cruelty and whose own son probably killed him.

Pyrrhus was the cruel son of Achilles and king of Spirus (an enemy of the Romans). Sextus was a sea pirate and the son of Pompey the Great. Attila is probably a reference to Attila the Hun, who was called the "Scourge of God." The Pazzian and Cornetan

Canto XII 55

Riniers were robbers of Dante's day.

Study Questions

1. Canto XII begins with a reference to a "Thing." What is this thing? Describe it.
2. What natural disaster or occurrence has happened since Virgil's trip to that area?
3. Who is the great Prince referred to in the Canto?
4. Who is the prey mentioned in Canto XII?
5. What is a centaur? Who is the leader or chief of the centaurs?
6. What is the task of the centaurs?
7. When they are walking together, Chiron reveals that he is aware of the fact that Dante is still alive. How does he know this?
8. When Chiron asks why Dante is there, how does Virgil respond to him?
9. Who are Nessus and Deianira?
10. At one point Virgil speaks of a woman who told him to bring Dante to Hell. Who is this woman?

Answers

1. The "Thing" is a Minotaur with the head of a bull and the body of a man.
2. A landslide has caused a rock to break in two and a wall to split.
3. The great Prince is a reference to Christ.
4. The prey is a reference to those taken from Hell by Christ.
5. A centaur has the head and upper torso of a man; the rest of its body is that of a horse. Chiron is the leader of the centaurs.
6. The centaurs use their bows and arrows to shoot those who try to raise themselves from the boiling blood.

7. Chiron knows that Dante is still alive because he can see that Dante's feet move the rocks and stones when Dante walks.
8. Virgil responds that necessity brings Dante to this place.
9. Nessus is the centaur who had attempted to steal Deianira, Hercules' wife.
10. The woman of whom Virgil speaks is Beatrice.

Suggested Essay Topics

1. Dante has crossed three rivers: the Acheron, the Styx, and the Phlegethon. Compare and contrast each of these rivers.
2. Explain the relationship of the sin of violence and the punishment of boiling them in the blood of the Phlegethon.

Canto XIII

New Characters:

Harpies: *Voracious creatures with bodies of birds and heads of women*

Bleeding Trees: *Trees containing the souls of suicide victims*

"Two that ran": *A reference to Lano of Siena (who sold his estates with other young men in a club and who wasted his money and life) and to Jacomo di Sant Andrea (who burned his own home for fun)*

Pier delle Vigne: *Accused of plotting against Fredrick II; took own life after being blinded and imprisoned; deemed guilty of only suicide—not betrayal—by Dante since in upper level*

Summary

Dante and Virgil find themselves in a dark forest which is not green but dark. In this forest are Harpies—creatures with the bodies of birds and the heads of women. Dante finds that the trees contain the spirits of those who were suicide victims. He listens to their stories of being imprisoned in the trees and of feeling pain

Canto XIII

when the leaves are plucked or the limbs broken. Dante recognizes some of these spirits; the one who held the key to Fredrick's heart tells Dante his sorrowful story, which is interrupted by the two hounded spirits "Two that ran."

Analysis

Originally in mythology the Harpies were personifications of the storm winds; later they became the bird-women with piercing cries.

Since those who have committed suicide had refused life, they are deprived of a human body in the pit. Since they used up their energy in life hating themselves, their energy is drained and their bodies are sapped of fertility. The dry, brittle trees which imprison them reflect this lack of energy, or sap.

In the Canto the "Two that ran" is a reference to both Lano of Siena and to Jacomo di Sant Andrea. Lano sold his estates, like the other young men in a club; he threw away this money and his life. Jacomo di Sant Andrea was also a member of this club; he burned his own home and the homes of others for amusement.

The "one who held the keys" is a reference to Pier delle Vigne, who was accused of plotting against Frederick II, in 1249. After being tortured, blinded, and imprisoned, Pier took his own life. Since Dante placed Pier in the upper level of the pit, he evidently deemed him guilty of only suicide—not betrayal.

Study Questions

1. In line 94 a reference is made to Minos. Who is Minos?
2. In line 64 a reference is made to a harlot. Who is this harlot?
3. Why is Dante reluctant to speak to the trees?
4. A reference is made in line 8 to a place between Corveto and Cecina. What does this mean?
5. Canto XIII concludes with a reference to the fact that the shade made a scaffold of his roof-tree. What does this mean?
6. Why does Virgil ask Dante to pluck a small branch or twig from a tree?

Canto XIII

7. Describe in detail the Harpies mentioned in Canto XIII.
8. In Canto XIII what comes forth from a tree in the woods if a branch is plucked?
9. What is meant by the phrase that suggests Florence changed her patron for the Baptist?
10. What do the Harpies eat?

Answers

1. Minos is a judge in the underworld.
2. The harlot is Envy.
3. Dante's heart is so filled with pity that he is reluctant to ask further questions.
4. The reference in line 8 is to a place between the River Cecina and the town of Corveto.
5. The one who made a scaffold of his roof-tree had committed suicide by hanging.
6. When Dante cannot decide from where the sounds in the forest are coming from, Virgil asks Dante to pluck from the tree.
7. The Harpies had bodies of birds, heads of women, sharp claws of steel, and shrieking voices.
8. Blood and voices come from a tree in the woods of Canto XIII when a branch is plucked.
9. The reference to the Baptist is a reference to John the Baptist, for whom a church in Florence is named.
10. The Harpies eat the foliage from the trees; this causes agony to the trees.

Suggested Essay Topics

1. Compare and contrast the woods in Canto XIII with the woods in Canto I, when Dante realizes he is lost.
2. Describe how the spirits of the suicide victims enter the trees.

Canto XIV

New Characters:

Blasphemers: *Includes Capaneus, one of seven kings in siege of Thebes*

Summary

Dante gathers the scattered leaves and places them about the tree to whom he is speaking; Dante and Virgil continue their journey.

They next find themselves in a desert pelted by a rain of fire; Dante speculates that Cato once marched here. They find the blasphemers. Virgil speaks with anger to Capaneus and compares his hot rage to the hot sands. The two travelers see a brook whose color is red near the sand. Virgil tells Dante that this brook puts out all flames.

Virgil tells Dante of the past days of Rhea and of the old man who stands on the mountain. Dante asks about the origin and the course of the rivers Lethe and Phlegethon. After Virgil answers, they continue on their journey.

Analysis

Dante's gathering of the leaves is significant of his love for his native city and the land from which the soul in the tree had come.

Cato's complete name was Marcus Porcius Cato the Younger; he was a Roman statesman who opposed the war between Caesar and Pompey but finally took sides with Pompey. After one battle he escaped and marched across the Libyan desert in 47 B.C. Rather than making peace with Caesar, he committed suicide.

Capaneus was one of those who participated in the war of the "Seven against Thebes." When he mocked the gods and boasted that not even Jove could stop him, a bolt of lightning struck him.

Rhea is a reference to the wife of Saturn and the mother of Jupiter. Saturn was fearful that his child would take over his role so he devoured his sons as they were born. Rhea allowed Jupiter to escape to a far place. The old man is a reference to the four ages of man: gold, silver, brass, and iron. Since people have not been perfect since the Golden Age, the statue is cracked.

Canto XIV 61

In his impromptu geography lesson, Virgil tells Dante of the River Lethe on the other side of the wall and of the Phlegethon which they had just passed. After the lesson which serves to orient both Dante and the reader, the two continue.

Study Questions

1. Why does Dante gather the leaves from the ground and place them back near the tree?
2. What is the symbolism of the rain of fire?
3. Who is Capaneus?
4. Who is Cato?
5. What is the name of the mountain?
6. What is the man made from?
7. Which river is able to put out the flames on either side?
8. What is one of the greatest marvels that Virgil tells Dante he will see?
9. Where does Rhea reside?
10. How does Virgil feel about the many questions Dante asked?

Answers

1. Dante gathers the leaves because he loves Italy.
2. The rain of fire refers to the words which blaspheme and shower down on others.
3. Capaneus is one who participated in the "Seven against Thebes"; when he insulted the gods and said that he was invincible, he was killed by a lightning bolt.
4. Cato's complete name is Marcus Porcius Cato the Younger; he was a Roman statesman who opposed the war between Caesar and Pompey but finally took sides with Pompey. After one battle he escaped and marched across the desert. Rather than making peace with Caesar, he committed suicide.

Canto XIV

5. The name of the mountain is Ida.
6. The man is made of gold, silver, brass, and iron.
7. The Phlegethon is able to put out the fire on either side of the stream.
8. Virgil tells Dante that the brook which is able to put out the fire on either side is an amazing sight.
9. Rhea resides in Crete.
10. Virgil is delighted with the questions which Dante asked him.

Suggested Essay Topics
1. Describe how the valley was made.
2. Describe some of the events that happened in Crete, according to the stories told by Virgil.

Canto XV

New Characters:

Violent against Nature: *Committed sins against the body and Nature; punished by running; includes Sodomites and alcoholics*

Summary

When the two continue their journey, Dante notes that the banks of the river are comparable to the dikes of Flanders and of Padua, Italy. They see the Violent against Nature who are running perpetually. One of these runners speaks and Dante sees that it is Brunetto Latini, a former adviser to Dante. They greet each other and converse; Dante thanks him and Brunetto predicts that Dante will be treated poorly by those in Florence. Latini notes Dante's merits and speaks ill of the injustice of Florence. Dante asks him who is there and, after naming a bishop transferred from Florence to Venice, Latini tells him to remember the books of Latini where Dante still lives.

Canto XV

Analysis

Those who are violent against Nature include the Sodomites; the rain (or aimless running) of these people is not fruitful but infertile much like the rain of fire on the desert. Dante is pleased to see his former teacher; Latini tells Dante not to give up even if he is ill-used by those in his home town of Florence. Latini tells Dante that Francis of Accorso and Priscian are there; Priscian had been a grammarian and Francis had been a lawyer. Latini believes that his books will preserve his memory.

Study Questions

1. With what does Dante compare the banks of the river as they continue their journey?
2. How long have Dante and Virgil been traveling?
3. Who is Brunetto?
4. How does Brunetto say that Dante can win?
5. What does Dante say that he will do with the words that Brunetto gives him?
6. Who is the wise lady that Dante mentions in the passage?
7. What is the meaning of the words "Well-heeded is well-heard"?
8. Why does the adviser not tell Dante who is in Circle VII?
9. Who is the "Servant of servants"?
10. How does Dante say that he feels about the future?

Answers

1. Dante compares the banks of the rivers with the dikes of Flanders and the dikes of Padua, Italy.
2. Dante and Virgil had left on Friday and the daylight of the day is fading. They talk through the dusk and the night until a new day dawns.
3. Brunetto was a former teacher/adviser to Dante.
4. Brunetto says that Dante could win by following his star.

5. Dante says that he will write down the words that Brunetto has shared with him and will give them to a wise lady.
6. The wise lady is a reference to Beatrice.
7. The words mean that what one really hears well is something that one obeys.
8. The adviser tells Dante that it will take too long to mention them all by name.
9. The "Servant of servants" is the Pope.
10. Dante says that he is unafraid about the future.

Suggested Essay Topics
1. What things does Dante share with his former adviser? What things does his former adviser share with him?
2. Go back through all the cantos up to this point. Find all the references to Beatrice and note the nouns that are used in place of her name. What do these references and nouns tell you about Dante's impressions of her?

Canto XVI

New Characters:

Three Florentines: *Ask Dante about Florence; now in Hell*

Summary

Near the waterfall Dante encounters three Florentines; they recognize Dante's dress as being Florentine. The three men were once nobles and one introduces them: Guido Guerra, Tegghiaio Aldobrandi, and Jacopo Rusticucci. Jacopo inquires of Florence; he explains that the shades have had concerns since Guillim Borsier' told them many tales. After Dante tells them of self-made men and excesses in Florence, they ask that he tell the living of them. As suddenly as they had come, the three run away.

The two travelers find that they are very close to the waterfalls. Dante compares the water to the Acquacheta and Forli

Canto XVI

(rivers) in the Apennines (mountains) of Italy. Oddly, Virgil removes Dante's rope girdle and throws it into the water. A shape in the water rises and engulfs the belt or sash.

Analysis

The three men who hail Dante recognize by his clothing that he is from Florence. Virgil informs Dante that the three who have just hailed him had been nobles in life. If they were not now in Hell, Virgil continues, Dante would have run to them, rather than vice versa, since he would admire them for their political virtues.

The three men are Guido Guerra, a Guelph who was noted for his sword and his counsel; Tegghiaio Aldobrandi, spokesperson for the Guelphs: and Jacopo Rusticucci, who was mentioned earlier in Canto VI, who was a Guelph of great wealth, and whose wife drove him into vice. They speak of the arrival of a Florentine named Guillim Borsier' who tells them of changes in the city. Borsier' was originally a purse maker but in his previous life, he began to "rub elbows" with the nobility. He helped them arrange marriages, make treaties, etc. Borsier' had shared the changes that he knew of while he and his fellow Florentines ran about in Circle VII. The shades request that when Dante is able to say that he *was* in Hell—but is there no longer—to mention their names to others.

The symbolism of the rope girdle is not immediately evident. Perhaps Virgil uses the rope girdle to draw the monster forth since the girdle is the only thing available to throw as a signal. Perhaps the rope—which Dante says was once intended to capture a leopard—is a symbol of the earlier sins of incontinence which continue to crop up in one's life. Dante was unable to capture a giant cat with the rope, but it is now used to draw forth a monster from the pit. The rope may also symbolize false hope that Virgil wants Dante to cast aside in favor of reason. There are many symbolic interpretations.

Canto VII has an open ending. The reader knows that some creature has come up from the depths of the water, but Dante does not reveal what that creature is.

Study Questions

1. What does Dante mean when he says that he has to fall to the center?
2. What do the three shades mean when they say that Guillim Borsier' has "but late enrolled"?
3. How does Dante feel about the three shades and their punishment in Hell?
4. What is the political affiliation of the three shades?
5. How does Virgil say that Dante is to treat the three shades?
6. What are the Acquacheta and the Forli?
7. What does Virgil throw into the water?
8. What are the Apennines?
9. Whom does Jacopo blame for his vice?
10. What is the Comedy that Dante refers to in Canto XVI?

Answers

1. When Dante says he has to fall to the center, he means that he has to continue his journey through the pit.
2. The three shades mean that Borsier' has just come to Hell when they say that he had recently enrolled.
3. Dante feels sadness that the shades are in Hell. His inclination is to keep the fire away even if he had to jump in himself but, of course, he cannot relieve their punishment.
4. The three shades belong to the Guelph party from Florence.
5. Virgil says that Dante is to treat the shades with courtesy.
6. The Acquacheta and the Forli are rivers.
7. Virgil throws the rope girdle from Dante's waist into the water.
8. The Apennines are mountains in Italy.
9. Jacopo blames his wife for his vice.
10. The Comedy that Dante refers to is his *Divine Comedy*.

Canto XVII

Suggested Essay Topics

1. Compare and contrast what is said of Jacopo Rusticucci in Canto VI and in Canto XVI.
2. Many of the persons whom Dante has seen in Hell have asked to be remembered to others when he returns from the pit. Why do you think that they make that request? Answer completely. You may give several reasons, but you must justify each.
3. Predict what you think will come from the pit where Virgil throws the rope girdle. Describe it in detail.

Canto XVII

New Characters:

Geryon: *The monster from the Circles of Fraud; also a monster killed by Hercules; part beast, part man, and part reptile*

Usurers: *Moneylenders who multiply luxuries at the expense of the earth and others; with Sodomites since both make a steril earth*

Summary

The monster Geryon which rises from the Circles of Fraud has a kindly face, the body of a snake, and hairy arms and paws. The two travelers must approach him, however, in order to continue their journey; to reach the Nether Region, they must descend on the creature's back.

Near the monster is a group of people on the sand. Virgil instructs Dante to talk with this unhappy lot. Dante notes that about their necks are purses; their eyes are fixed on these objects and on the ground. As they cry, one speaks to Dante. He tells how the Florentines kept shouting for a knight with a satchel bearing three goats. Dante, fearing to keep his host too long, rushes back to Virgil.

Virgil tells Dante to take courage while they mount Geryon, which they must ride to the depths below them. Dante compares their ride with that of Phaeton when he drove his sun-chariot across the sky and of Icarus who flew too near the sun with his wings of feathers and wax.

Upon depositing the travelers, Geryon departs quickly. The pair are ready to continue their journey through Hell.

Analysis

Dante notes the nearby Usurers on the ground. The purses about their necks bear the signs of their families and their coat of arms; they look toward their purses, their first love. They look toward the hot ground (or Nature) which God intended that they use for a livelihood and which they spurned. These burned creatures share the same area of Hell with the Sodomites, who also make the earth sterile. The person with the goats upon his satchel whom the Usurers seek is Satan; the Scriptures speak of Judgment Day when God shall separate the sheep from the goats. The goats will go to Dis with Satan; Satan bears this symbol on his satchel. It is logical that those in the fiery pit should seek the ruler of their abode.

Study Questions
1. Why does Virgil tell Dante to talk with those in the Circles of Fraud?
2. Describe the sounds that Dante hears while riding the creature from the depths.
3. What part of the Geryon does Dante consider dangerous?
4. To what animal does Dante compare the Usurers?
5. What do the Usurers wear about their throats?
6. What is on the purses of the Usurers?
7. What are the faces of the Usurers like? Why are they like that?
8. How do Dante and Virgil get to the next circle?
9. How does Dante feel on the trip to the next circle?
10. Who was Icarus? How does Dante's fear compare with Icarus's fear?

Answers

1. Virgil wants Dante to learn all he can about this ring.
2. Dante hears the noise of the cataracts to the right and the wails from the pit.
3. The Geryon's tail is a venomed fork.
4. Dante compares the Usurers to dogs.
5. The Usurers wear purses about their throats.
6. The coats of arms of their families are on the Usurers' purses.
7. The faces of the Usurers are burned and scarred. The hot ground has burned their faces because they spurned making a living by Nature (or the arts) and concentrated on money lending.
8. Dante and Virgil get to the next circle on the back of the Geryon.
9. Dante is very frightened on the trip to the next circle.
10. Icarus flew with wings made of wax and feathers; he flew too near the sun and the wax melted. Dante's fear as he approaches the pit is equal to Icarus's as he approached the earth in his fall.

Suggested Essay Topics

1. Describe in detail the creature that comes from the Circle of Fraud. Does it seem an appropriate monster for the Circle of Fraud? Explain your answer.
2. Compare and contrast the levels of sin and punishment of those in the boiling river of blood, the fiery rain, and the burning sand.

Canto XVIII

New Characters:

Venedico Caccianemico: *Member of the Guelphs who sold his own sister*

72   The Divine Comedy I: Inferno

Horned Fiends: *Those who beat the naked sinners in the Malbowges*

Jason: *Greek hero who searched for the golden fleece and seduced others*

Alessio Interminei: *A White Guelph; a flatterer with "slick" manners*

Summary

Dante describes the region in Hell called the Malbowges, or Evil Pockets. He explains that this area is made of iron-gray stone and has ten divisions. In the middle of this cone, or narrowing round, is a well. Dante describes how the traffic of the souls in the Malbowges is controlled: one side keeps their eyes on the Castle (perhaps the Castle on the road called the Castello Sant' Angelo) and the other side keeps their eyes on the Mount (perhaps the mountain called Janiculum).

Dante observes the naked sinners and the horned fiends who beat them and drive them along with heavy whips. The trail moves in opposite ways; the first procession is composed of panders and the second procession is composed of seducers. Dante recognizes Venedico Caccianemico coming from one direction and Jason moving from the other direction.

Dante sees, deep in the trench, people submerged in filth. One of these persons is Alessio Interminei; this former resident of Lucca explains that flatteries brought him here. Virgil also recognizes the harlot Thais in this trench.

Analysis

"In the gutter," or in the trenches of Malbowges, one finds the disintegration of human beings, the city, and morals. The depths of the trenches reflects how far human beings have sunk sexually, morally, and even in words—such as flatterers. The flatterers in the trench include Alessio Interminei and the harlot Thais—both are being punished for their sins with words—and deeds.

Dante recognizes Venedico Caccianemico, a Guelph and a pander who sold his own sister to Obizzo d' Este of Ferrara (Canto XII). From the other direction he recognizes Jason of the Argonauts,

Canto XVIII

a seducer who married and deserted Medea and who lured Hypsipyle after she rescued her father from Lemnos.

The flatterers in the trench include Alessio Interminei and the harlot Thais; both are here only for their sins with words. (Thais is not here for her prostitution.)

Study Questions

1. What is Malbowges? Of what is Malbowges made? What is in the middle of Malbowges?
2. Compare and contrast seducers and panders.
3. Why is Alessio Interminei in this place?
4. How many parts are in Malbowges?
5. What is a bowge?
6. Of what sins are those in the first and second parts of Malbowges guilty?
7. How are these seducers being punished?
8. On which side of the road do the sinners walk?
9. How are the flatterers punished?
10. For what sin is the harlot being punished?

Answers

1. Malbowges is a region in Hell made of iron-gray stone with a well in the middle.
2. One who lures or stimulates others into sin is a seducer; one who panders may sell or exploit sin.
3. Alessio Interminei is in Malbowges because of his sins of flattery.
4. There are ten parts in Malbowges.
5. A bowge is a trench.
6. Those in the first and second parts of Malbowges are guilty of seduction and flattery.
7. Horned fiends with whips are beating the seducers.

8. Sinners walk on the right side of the road in Malbowges.
9. The flatterers were submerged in dung.
10. The harlot is being punished for the sin of flattery.

Suggested Essay Topics
1. Dante opens Canto XVIII with a descriptive passage unequaled anywhere else in the *Inferno*. What does he describe? Why does he spend so much time on this description?
2. Dante seems to be drawn to heroes. What hero is described in Canto XVIII? Why is he placed in Malbowges? What trait(s) does he have that Dante admires? Explain your answer.

Canto XIX

New Characters:

Simoniacs: *Include Pope Nicholas III; profited from sale of holy items*

Summary

This canto begins with a reference to Simon Magus and his disciples who have sold the things of God for profit.

Dante describes those in the Third Bowge (Trench) of the Malbowges; he sees holes in the banks and grounds where only the feet of the sinners are showing. The feet of these shades are on fire; their joints quiver with pain. When Dante asks whom he is seeing, Virgil asks Dante to follow him and they will go to the lower bank so that Dante can see for himself what is going on in the holes.

Dante addresses one of these sinners; the sinner addresses Dante as Boniface and reminds "Boniface" that he betrayed the Fairest among Women. Dante admits, at the insistence of Virgil, that he is not Boniface. The sinner explains that he once wore the Great Mantle and was the son of the Bear. In his previous life this former Pope wanted to advance his litter and placed his coins in a pouch up above and placed himself in a pouch down below.

Canto XIX 75

The Pope in Hell refers to Boniface VIII as being a Jason; Dante responds with the question of how many coins God required of Peter and Matthias. Dante goes on to remind Pope Nicholas that "she" sits on the floods; he also mentions the numbers seven and ten. Dante calls on Constantine and watches the Pope wiggle his feet with all his power.

After praising Dante for his words to the shade, Virgil leads him on the rest of the journey.

Analysis

Simon Magus in the Book of Acts is the person for whom the sin of simony was named. One who simonizes sells the holy articles of God for profit. Dante sees their punishment: they are placed head down in a hole and their feet are burned. The holes are similar to those that priests stand in to perform baptisms.

The sinner in the hole (a Pope) believes that Pope Boniface VIII betrayed the Church (the Fairest among Women) by selling holy items and is there for punishment. Dante finds that the Popes are stacked on top of each other and that there is only one hole for Popes.

The sinner in the hole (Pope Nicholas III) tells Dante that he once wore the Great Mantle, another name for the Papal Cloak, and was the Son of the Bear, a reference to his family name of Orsini which means "bear." He is now in a pouch or hole just as his coins from selling holy items were in a pouch before his death.

Jason is a reference to one who bought his position in the Church. Dante reminds Pope Nicholas III that Jesus required no money from the disciples in order for them to follow him; no money was required of Matthias, who took Judas's place after Judas betrayed Jesus and hanged himself.

The reference to seven is to the Seven Sacraments and the reference to ten is to the Ten Commandments. The reference to Constantine is to the Christian Emperor who allegedly transferred his rule over Italy to the Papal See.

Study Questions

1. How does Dante know that Virgil approves of what he says?
2. Who is Simon Magus?

Canto XIX

3. Why does Dante break up an area made for the priests to stand in to perform baptisms?
4. What is the punishment of the Simoniacs?
5. What is the punishment of the priests?
6. Who is the priest with whom Dante speaks?
7. For whom does Nicholas III mistake Dante?
8. Who is the "Fairest among Women" that the priests had used poorly?
9. Why does Nicholas III not realize that Dante is not Pope Boniface VIII?
10. Who is the disciple who replaces Judas?

Answers

1. Dante knows that Virgil approves of his words because 1) he smiles when Dante speaks and 2) he clasps him to his breast when Dante finishes speaking.
2. Simon Magus had sold holy items for profit.
3. When a child becomes caught in the area made for priests to stand in, Dante breaks up the area.
4. The Simoniacs are head-down in the holes with fire burning their feet.
5. The priests are placed on top of each other in the same hole.
6. The priest with whom Dante speaks is Nicholas III.
7. Nicholas III mistakes Dante for Pope Boniface VIII.
8. The woman whom the priests had used poorly is the Church.
9. Nicholas III does not recognize that Dante is not Pope Boniface VIII because Pope Nicholas's head is buried in the hole.
10. The disciple who replaces Judas is Matthias.

Suggested Essay Topics

1. Explain the relationship between the sin of trafficking in holy articles and the punishment in Hell.
2. How does the punishment of Popes differ from the punishment of ordinary people in this area of Hell?

Canto XX

New Characters:

Sinners with Their Heads on Backwards: *Astrologers, sorcerers, and magicians; represented by Michael Scott, Asdante, and Guy Bonatti*

Summary

Dante describes the sinners with their heads on backwards and how he was moved to pity and to weeping upon seeing them. Virgil, on the other hand, reprimands Dante for crying and asks who could be more wicked than one who is tormented here.

Virgil refers to Amphiaraus and Tiresias in his speech telling of the origin of Mantua. Some of the people whom Dante sees just before he and Virgil leave the area are Michael Scott, Asdante, and Guy Bonatti.

Analysis

The punishment for trying to predict the future is to be forced to look forever backward. These shades have no hope for the future. Another interpretation for this punishment is that fortune telling, sorcery, and magic are contorted arts.

Virgil's question of who is more wicked than one who is tormented has a double meaning. It can mean no one is more wicked than those whom God must chastise; it can mean no one is more wicked than those who are tormented by seeing God's justice meted out in Hell.

Amphiaraus saw his death and tried to leave a battle only to be killed by an earthquake. Tiresias was also a prophet; he changes

Canto XX

himself into the shape of a woman; then he broke the spell seven years later and became a man again. Michael Scott was a magician; Asdante, a soothsayer; and Guy Bonatti, an astrologer.

Study Questions

1. Dante mentions the Abyss and the chasm; to what is he referring?
2. What is unusual about the sinners that Dante sees in Canto XX?
3. Amphiaraus tried to look ahead to save his own life; what happens to him when he leaves a battle?
4. What does Tiresias strike with his wand?
5. What happens to Tiresias after he uses his wand the first time in striking these objects?
6. How does Tiresias change himself back after using his wand the first time?
7. What is the crime of the sinners who have their heads turned backwards on their bodies?
8. Who is the daughter of Tiresias?
9. At about what speed do those with their heads twisted on their necks move?
10. On what day of the week do all these events occur?

Answers

1. Dante is referring to Hell when he makes mention of the Abyss and the chasm.
2. The sinners have their heads twisted backwards.
3. When Amphiaraus tries to save his own life by leaving a battle, he is killed by an earthquake.
4. Tiresias strikes his wand upon twin and tangled snakes.
5. Upon using his wand to strike the twin and tangled snakes the first time, Tiresias becomes a woman.

6. Tiresias strikes the twin snakes with his wand again to turn back into a man.
7. Those with their heads turned backwards are guilty of predicting the future.
8. The daughter of Tiresias is Manto.
9. Those with heads twisted on their necks move at a slow pace; their speed is likened to that of the slow walk of a Litany procession.
10. All these events happen on the Saturday before Easter.

Suggested Essay Topics

1. Why are the sinners that Dante observed in Canto XX punished by having their heads turned backwards?
2. Explain what Virgil means when he says that in Hell either piety or pity must die.

Canto XXI

New Characters:

Barrators: *Sinners who made money in public office*

Demons: *Include Hacklespur, Hellkin, Harrowhound, Libbicock, Dragonel, Barbinger, Grabbersnitch, Rubicant, Farfarel, Belzecue*

Summary

The Fifth Bowge is dark and filled with the bubbles of boiling pitch; to prevent the sinners from drawing themselves from the pitch, demons keep pushing them down, much as a cook stirs a cooking pot of stew to make sure all bits and pieces in the pot are submerged.

Virgil suddenly pulls Dante aside and cries, "Look out!" A winged demon, carrying an alderman, is moving quickly behind Dante. This alderman is a barrator, who made money from hidden deals and from grabbing money in secret.

Virgil instructs Dante to hide and wait; Virgil confronts the demons directly and explains that he and Dante must pass. The demons summon another of their numbers; this demon, named Belzecue, protects them and allows them to pass.

Belzecue tells them that five hours from this time (minus one day) will mark the time that an earthquake occurred 1266 years ago. This quake destroyed a bridge without which passage will be difficult. Belzecue tells the two travelers that he will send some demons to protect them as they travel.

Dante is reluctant to have these companions, but Virgil says that the grimaces the demons make are intended for the sinners and not for them. As the two travelers leave, they see the demons stick out their tongues at Belzecue, who plays a bugle as they leave.

Analysis

The sinners in this trench are punished by darkness, pitch, and demons with forks. Just as money stuck to the fingers of the barrators in life, so the boiling pitch will stick to them as punishment in Hell. The barrators are confined to darkness to symbolize their black, evil deeds that were done under cover.

The earthquake that Belzecue mentions occurred at the time that Christ died on the cross; most experts believe that the death came at 3:00 p.m. If death was at 3:00 p.m., as the gospels declare, then the contact with Belzecue occurred at 10:00 a.m.

Dante's apprehension about the demons who will accompany them is foreshadowing of later occurrences as Belzecue gives them false directions in order to entrap them. When the journey recommences, the demons bid each other good-bye by sticking out their tongues. Belzecue trumpets good-bye with a loud cry.

Study Questions

1. Why does Virgil pull Dante to one side and cry out?
2. What is a barrator?
3. Why do the barrators remain in the boiling pitch?
4. How does Virgil manage to get by and to help Dante get by the demons?

Canto XXI 83

5. What is the name of the main demon?
6. Describe the appearance of the demons.
7. What caused the earthquake that destroyed the bridge?
8. On what day of the week does the encounter with Belzecue occur?
9. What year did the earthquake occur?
10. What time of day is it as the demons talk with Dante and Virgil?

Answers
1. Virgil pulls Dante to one side and cries out because he sees a demon with an alderman in his arms.
2. A barrator is one who makes money through public office; usually undercover deals and secret money-taking is involved in such profit.
3. The barrators remain in the boiling pitch because demons torture them if they emerge.
4. Virgil has Dante hide until he says to come out; Virgil speaks to the demon and explains their presence.
5. The name of the main demon is Belzecue.
6. The demons have wings, high-hunched shoulders, and hideous hooks.
7. The earthquake occurred at the death of Christ.
8. The encounter with Belzecue takes place on Saturday.
9. The earthquake occurred in the year 1266.
10. It is about 10:00 a.m. when the demons talk with Dante and Virgil.

Suggested Essay Topics
1. Describe in detail the sights and sounds of the Fifth Bowge, or the Fifth Trench. Compare and contrast these with another canto and the sights and sounds witnessed there.

Canto XXII

2. Discuss the punishments for the sinners in the Fifth Bowge. Do you think these punishments are related to the sin? Why did you answer as you did?

Canto XXII

New Character:

The Soul from Navarre: *Probably Gian Polo; Spaniard; former servant*

Summary

Dante says that the many sights and sounds of his past do not compare with the journey that he is now beginning. Dante sees sinners jumping into the hot-pot to escape the wrath of the demons; one soul, however, does not submerge himself and is hooked by a demon. This soul is from Navarre and tells of events in his life; after his narrative the demons torture the shade.

The soul tells of others who occupy the pit with him: Fra Gomita and Don Michael Zanche. He makes a deal with the demons to fetch up seven to substitute for himself. The demons threaten to come after him if he fails to deliver. When the demons look away, the soul dives into the pit.

This trickery causes the demons to squabble among themselves. While they argue, splutter in rage, and fight among themselves, Dante and Virgil slip away.

Analysis

Dante is horrified and amazed at the sights he sees. The soul that does not return promptly to the pit may be Gian Polo, a Spaniard, from Navarre. Fra Gomita, who was hanged, was at one time a judge of the province of Gallura. Don Michael Zanche was a son of Fredrick II; his son-in-law murdered him in 1290. Canto XXXIII refers to Branca d'Oria, the murderer of Zanche.

The trickery employed by Gian Polo illustrates a common literary theme: survival of the unfittest; technically the least fit should not conquer, but the survival and conquest of the "underdog" makes for interesting reading. The two travelers—Dante and Virgil—continue on their journey; their actions depict a second traditional theme: that of the journey, called the picaresque theme.

Study Questions

1. What is the legend of the dolphins mentioned in Canto XXII?
2. What is the reaction of the shades to Barbiger?
3. What is the name of the shade who does not submerge himself?
4. How do Dante and Virgil manage to get rid of their escort?
5. How do the demons punish Gian Polo when they find him out of the pitch?
6. What does Gian Polo promise to bring back from the pit?
7. Gian Polo is from which kingdom?
8. To which animals does Dante compare those in the pitch?
9. From which country does Gian Polo come?
10. What signal do the shades use to tell the others that the coast is clear?

Answers

1. The legend mentioned in Canto XXII is that of dolphins' warning those at sea of storms.
2. The shades are frightened of Barbiger.
3. The shade who does not submerge himself promptly is Gian Polo.
4. Dante and Virgil manage to get rid of their escort when the demons begin to fight among themselves.
5. The demons pull him up on a hook and rip off parts of his body.
6. Gian Polo promises to bring others back from the pit with him.
7. Gian Polo is from the kingdom of Navarre.

Canto XXIII

8. Dante compares the people in the pit to dolphins and frogs.
9. Gian Polo is from Spain.
10. The shades whistle when the coast is clear.

Suggested Essay Topics

1. Dante inserts some humor, or comic relief, in Canto XXII when the demons are outwitted by one of the shades. Describe this event.
2. Compare the trickery used in Canto XXII with another story that you have read.

Canto XXIII

New Characters:

Hypocrites: *Wear cloaks with hoods, bright colors, and lead linings*

Catalano and Loderingo: *Two hooded friars from Bologna*

Caiaphas: *High priest; condemned Christ; crucified in Hell by triple stake*

Summary

Dante and Virgil continue their journey single file. Dante recalls a story from Aesop of a frog and a mouse; these thoughts occupy his mind for a while, and he has a feeling of fear of the demons in the back of his mind. When he expresses his concern, Virgil admits similar fears. The two travelers now see the demons swooping low as if trying to snatch up the pair.

Dante and Virgil flee to the next trench and see the hypocrites with their brightly painted hoods which are lined with lead. Two of the hypocrites who had been Jovial Friars ask about Dante and then introduce themselves as Catalano and Loderingo. Catalano explains that the crucified sinner on the ground was one who had given advice to the Pharisees.

Virgil asks directions and the hypocrite tells them the way to go. Virgil says that the one who uses a spear to hook the sinners must have given them bad advice. The two move on and Dante senses anger in Virgil.

Analysis

The story from Aesop which Dante recalls is one about a frog who ties a mouse to his leg in order to carry it across the water. The frog dives deep into the pond and the mouse drowns; a hawk swoops down and devours both. This story gives a sense of foreboding to the canto and adds to the reader's fear for the main characters. In some versions of the story the mouse is able to escape, but the reader is not sure which version will apply in this instance. There is foreshadowing from the beginning of the canto, however, so the reader is not surprised when the two travelers suddenly see the demons swoop low on their wide wings and try to seize them.

To escape the demons, the two travelers must hurry to the next trench. There they see the hooded hypocrites, but the capes, like the sinners wearing them, are not as they seem. The capes are brightly painted but lined with heavy lead. (Some authorities consider the paint as having been applied to the hypocrites themselves and not to the capes or hoods, but the later references to the "orange-gilded dress" and to the fact that "they were gilded dazzling-bright" seem to imply the capes—not the people themselves—were painted.)

The Jovial Friars (to which Catalano and Loderingo once belonged) was a religious group of knights with the official name of Ordo militiae beatae Mariae. The group had sought for about five years to protect the helpless and to bring peace, but its rules were quite lax and it did not survive. Catalano explains to Dante that the sinner that they see crucified is Caiaphas, the high priest who had condemned Christ to death.

Virgil asks directions from the two hypocrites and says that the demons have given him bad advice. The two leave to continue their journey and Dante follows in the prints of the beloved feet— perhaps an allusion to the fact that he and Virgil are following in the steps of Christ.

Canto XXIII

Study Questions

1. Why does Dante say that he is particularly frightened of the demons?
2. Is Dante alone in his fear?
3. What is Virgil's reaction when he sees the demons?
4. Who are the sinners in Circle VIII, Bowge VI?
5. How are they attired?
6. Who is the shade Dante sees crucified?
7. What is the formation that Virgil and Dante take when they resume travel?
8. Who are Catalano and Loderingo?
9. How are the demons able to overtake the two travelers if the travelers have a head start?
10. How long are the hypocrites to wear the cloaks?

Answers

1. Dante says that he is particularly frightened that the demons may become angry; because of Virgil and Dante, the demons have been tricked, made fools of, and knocked about. If the element of rage is added, the demons will probably come looking for them.
2. Dante is not alone in his fear; Virgil is also fearful.
3. Virgil becomes protective of Dante when he sees the demons.
4. The sinners in Circle VIII, Bowge VI are the hypocrites.
5. The hypocrites wear brightly colored cloaks lined with lead.
6. The shade who has been crucified is the high priest who had condemned Christ to the crucifixion.
7. Virgil walks ahead and Dante follows in his footsteps.
8. Loderingo and Catalano are two Jovial Friars.
9. By flying, the demons are able to overtake the travelers.
10. The hypocrites must wear the cloaks for eternity.

Suggested Essay Topics
1. An allegory is a text that has hidden spiritual meanings; using Canto XXIII, find any spiritual meanings you can and comment on each.
2. Dante refers to Aesop's fables. Research who Aesop was. Were all of Aesop's stories? Did Aesop write long before Dante? What are some other stories that Aesop wrote? Could Dante have incorporated any of these into his cantos?

Canto XXIV

New Character:

Vanni Fucci from Pistoia: *A thief; a runner from the serpents in the trench; predicts the future to hurt Dante*

Summary

The poets continue their journey. Dante is glad when Virgil's anger cools and they can continue the journey in a more pleasing manner. Virgil continues to help Dante and to give advice as they go; Dante heeds his recommendations.

In looking down into the pit, the two see only blackness. Dante suggests descending further so that he can look below. When they are finally able to see in the chasm of the seventh trench, the two see serpents of all types. Naked shades run terrified in their midst; the hands of these runners are tied behind their backs with snakes; the heads and tails of these snakes writhe at either side of the runners. One runner is stung and burns to ashes. His ashes resume his former state and he comes to talk with the two travelers.

The shade describes to Virgil and Dante the life he led as a beast instead of a person. The runner, whose name is Vanni Fucci from Pistoia, admits his shame at being found in this place and of his sins of stealing. Fucci predicts that Pistoia will change from the Blacks and that a new political party will take over the cities of Florence and Pistoia. Then he mentions that Mars shall bring "vapor" and the result will be a blow against the Whites. He readily admits that he tells Dante this to break Dante's heart.

Analysis

Dante knows Virgil well enough to be able to identify the emotions that the guide is experiencing. Virgil and Dante move closer to the pit to see what lies in the gloom and they see thieves cast among serpents.

Vanni Fucci confesses his shame and sin at being caught. This creeping thief Fucci is like the creeping serpent. Fucci tells them of the coming battle in which the Whites of Florence will assist the Whites of Pistoia in ousting the Blacks from Pistoia. He refers to a battle in which the Blacks are led by the vapor stack (Moroello Malaspina), the Lord of Lunigiana in the Valdimagra. Fucci tells Dante that Mars (the God of War) shall bring new battles and that the Whites shall be overcome.

To push the insult further, Fucci admits that he is sharing this information to hurt Dante. His information is like the bite of an adder.

Study Questions

1. What is a hind?
2. Describe the relationship between Dante and Virgil.
3. Virgil warns Dante several times to make sure that the rocks he steps on will bear his weight. Dante is not worried about this. Why?
4. What is Virgil's reaction to Dante's stopping for breath?
5. What does Dante see in Bowge VII with the sinners?
6. How are the sinners in Bowge VII tied?
7. What is Vanni Fucci's disposition?
8. Vanni Fucci refers to Mars. Who is Mars?
9. Fucci predicts the defeat of a faction? Which faction is this?
10. Why does Fucci share this prediction with Dante?

Answers

1. A hind is a farm assistant.
2. Virgil senses Dante's concern and smiles at him; Dante feels

Canto XXV

distress when his master is concerned. Virgil opens his arms to Dante; Virgil's action shows a love and friendship for Dante.

3. Dante is not worried about rocks bearing his weight because he reasons that if the hypocrites with cloaks of lead can walk on the rocks, his weight should not be a problem.
4. Virgil chastises Dante and urges him to continue moving down the path.
5. Dante sees serpents in Bowge VII with the sinners.
6. The sinners in Bowge VII are tied up with snakes.
7. Vanni Fucci is an ill-tempered brute.
8. Mars is the god of war.
9. Fucci predicts the defeat of the Whites.
10. Fucci shares with Dante his prophesy of the defeat of the Whites to break Dante's heart.

Suggested Essay Topics

1. How is the punishment of being placed in a chasm with vipers fitting punishments for those who steal?
2. Many interpreters see within Dante's writings a British Farm Association. Do you see such an association? Why? Justify your answer.

Canto XXV

New Characters:

Cacus: *Dragon with spread wings and breath of fire*

Five Spirits: *Florentine noblemen who (except for Puccio) change to animal shapes; include Agnello dei Brunelleschi, Cianfa die Donate, Buoso Degli Abati, Francesco Guercio dei Cavalcanti, and Puccio dei Galigai*

Summary

Vanni Fucci, the thief, makes a rude gesture and blasphemes; even the snakes seem to try to prevent Fucci from his actions. Dante admits pleasure at the placement of Fucci in the Inferno at this point and says that on his journey he has seen no other shade so defiant toward God. Pursued by an angry centaur, Vanni leaves at this point. On the back of the centaur, Dante sees a dragon with spread wings and fiery breath; Virgil tells him that this creature is Cacus.

Three spirits appear. One inquires as to who the two travelers are and Virgil and Dante pause in their conversation to reply. Dante hears one spirit ask the other why the spirit Cianfa lingers; Dante warns Virgil by a finger over the mouth to be cautious in his comments.

Suddenly a six-legged worm appears and leaps upon one of the spirits with its claws outstretched. The two join together and one head becomes two; two faces become one. The new creature reels away just as a lizard comes and jumps upon one of the others. The lizard pierces the mouth of the spirit. The spirit seems to yawn; smoke pours out of the mouth of the spirit and merges with the smoke from the lizard. A lizard becomes a man and a man becomes a brute before Dante's eyes; the man turns to say that he wants to see Buoso crawl as he had crawled. The spirit Puccio is the only one of the five spirits who does not undergo a metamorphosis. These sights remind Dante of tales he has read, but the tales do not compare with what he sees.

Analysis

It is evident from the beginning of this canto that the shame that Fucci professes in Canto XXIV is shame at being caught and not shame from remorse. Even the demons express anger toward Vanni Fucci.

The next portion of the canto is a description of a scene which Dante observes as spirits, serpents, and lizards changing their forms before him.

Agnello dei Brunelleschi is a spirit who becomes blended with Cianfa die Donate, a six-legged creature. Buoso Degli Abati appears first as a man and changes shapes with another—Francesco

Canto XXV

Guercio dei Cavalcanti, who appears first as a serpent. Puccio dei Galigai, the only spirit which does not undergo a transformation, is easily recognizable by Dante because he moves with a limp as he exits the scene. All five of the spirits were at one time nobles in Florence.

During the scene Dante remembers tales of others changing shapes. When Cato marched across the desert, Sabellus and Nasidius were stung by scorpions; Sabellus turned to water and Nasidius swelled to such an extent that he broke the mail on his body. Like Ovid, the ancient Roman poet who wrote *Metamorphoses*, told of Cadmus (who became a serpent after killing Mars' sacred serpent) and Arethusa (a nymph who was changed by Diane of the Hunt to a fountain), Dante tells his readers of what he sees.

Dante does not give all the details because of his confused, blurred vision, of the rapid speed of transformation, and his distraught mind. He will later use this guise again as he unravels to the reader the rest of his trip through *The Inferno*.

Study Questions

1. Fucci makes a sign at the beginning of the canto. What kind of sign is this?
2. At whom does Fucci make the gesture?
3. How does Dante feel about Fucci after observing his actions?
4. What does Dante believe is unique about Fucci?
5. What is Maremma?
6. Do you think that Fucci feels remorse for the sins he committed in life?
7. What is Cacus?
8. Where does Cacus live?
9. What does the term *metamorphosis* mean?
10. How does Dante recognize Puccio?

Canto XXV

Answers
1. Fucci makes a rude gesture at the beginning of the canto.
2. Fucci makes the gesture at God.
3. Dante dislikes Fucci intensely and does not regret that he is being punished.
4. Dante believes that Fucci is the most defiant spirit against God he has ever seen.
5. Maremma is a swampy area near Tuscany.
6. Fucci's actions in Hell do not indicate that he is a changed person so he evidently does not feel remorse; he seems sorry that he is caught.
7. Cacus is a dragon with spread wings and fiery breath.
8. Cacus lives beneath the high rock of Mount Aventine.
9. A *metamorphosis* is a change from one creature to another.
10. Dante recognizes Puccio because he limps.

Suggested Essay Topics
1. Compare and contrast Dante's attitude and feelings toward Vanni Fucci and his attitude and feelings toward the soothsayers and fortune tellers in Canto XX. Why do you think there is a change?
2. Dante does not reveal to the reader the step-by-step process in all the changes of man and beast in Canto XXV. How does he manage to omit some of these steps? Do you think that this omission weakens the canto? Explain your answer.

Canto XXVI

New Characters:

Counselors of Fraud: *Sinners who convince others to practice fraud; spiritual thieves who rob others of integrity*

The Dual Flame: *Ulysses and Diomede; planned the Trojan horse*

Summary

Dante appears to praise Florence because its reputation is scattered across land, water, and Hell. Dante refers to the bitter favor which Prato wanted for the city.

As they move on the stairs, Dante reflects that he must curb his "hot spirit" so as to use wisely his good gifts. Ahead Dante sees the Eighth Trench with its fires. These spires of flame come from the bodies of each thief below. While Dante watches, he nearly falls but is saved by Virgil.

Dante asks who walks in the tall, fiery spire he sees, and Virgil answers that it is Eteocles and his brother who had killed one another in a battle. Virgil also recognizes Ulysses and Diomede.

Virgil says that Dante should not talk to these spirits. Instead Virgil will ask the questions since he can sense Dante's thoughts and can speak to the Greeks who may spurn the language spoken by Dante.

Ulysses tells of his love of travel which not even his wife, his son, or his aging father could quell. On the sea voyage he recounts, his ship made good speed and he saw many things. He observed the "other pole" by night; five times the light kindled and waned. Foul weather struck, a whirlwind hit, and the seas closed over the ship.

Analysis

Dante is actually being sarcastic when he praises Florence for its reputation because its reputation is not all good and, therefore, extends to Hell—where many of its citizens dwell. Even the Church, through Cardinal Nicholas of Prato, cursed Florence; Pope Benedict XI had sent the Cardinal to Florence in hopes of bringing together the hostile political factions. The Cardinal gave up on Florence and

Canto XXVI

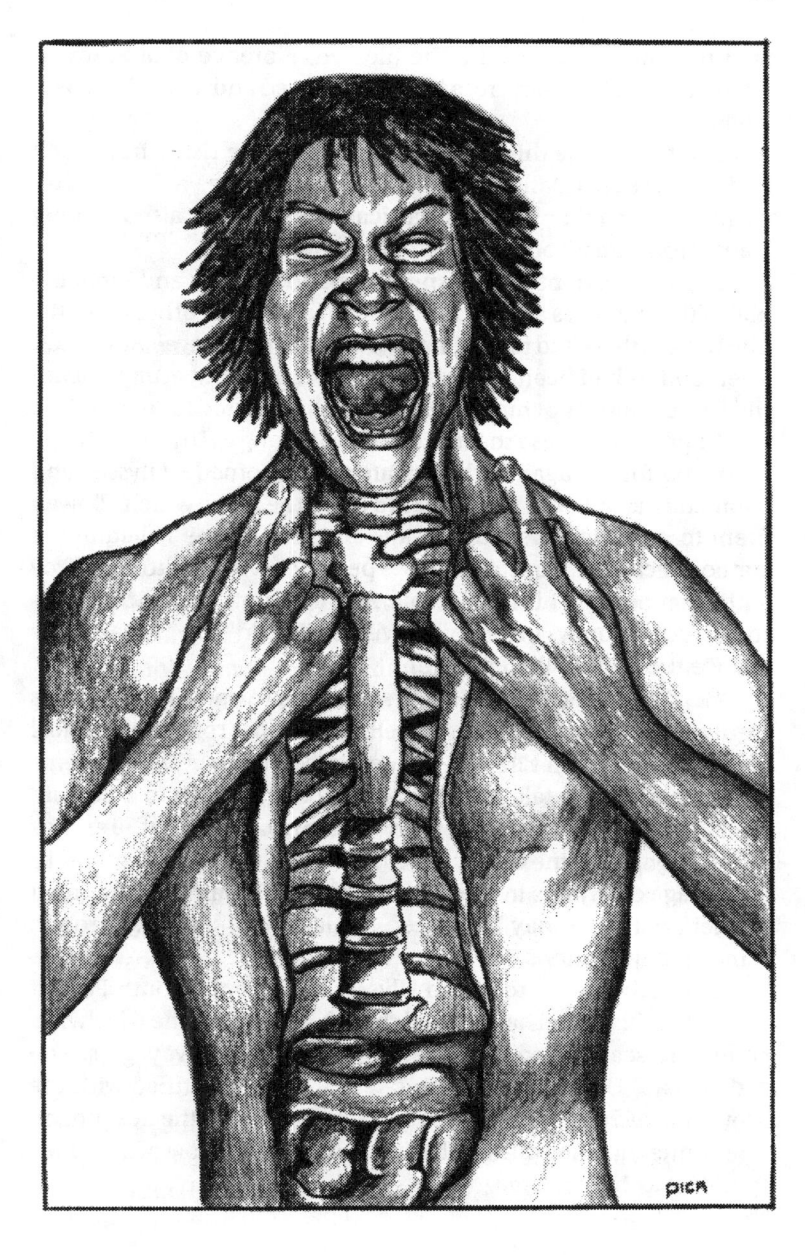

said that since it refused to be blessed, Florence could remain cursed. After his departure, a bridge collapsed and a fire killed over 2,000.

Dante sees the thieves with a spire of flame rising from each body. Virgil saves Dante from the fall; this could be a literal statement, but it could also be allegorical since Virgil is also rescuing Dante from the woods in which he was lost.

Dante questions whose spire burns so brightly and Virgil explains that Eteocles and his brother had killed each other in battle. The two brothers had fought in the war of the Seven against Thebes. Their bodies had been placed on a funeral pyre, but even in death the flames would not merge because of their hatred for each other.

Virgil explains also that the dual fires belong to Ulysses, a Greek hero who fought against the Trojans, and Diomede; Ulysses and Diomede had advised the Greeks to build the horse which allowed them to go inside the Trojan walls and to steal the Palladium, a statue which kept Troy safe. Ulysses persuades Achilles to go to Troy with Diomede and him; Deidamia, Achilles' mother, dies from sorrow since she knows that Achilles will be killed in Troy. These deaths avenge the theft of the Palladium.

Virgil conjures the spire of Ulysses to speak, and Ulysses speaks through the flame. The story he tells is not one from any classical source; rather it is a tale that Dante himself wrote. Ulysses seems to be recounting a tale rather than speaking directly to a person. The tale that Ulysses tells may have come from Homer, the author of the *Odyssey*. Some critics believe that this story refers to the final voyage of Ulysses in the *Odyssey*. Although Dante did not read Homer's work, he may have been familiar with this tale through translated quotations.

The "other pole" to which Ulysses refers is the South Pole; it seems that his vessel has crossed the equator. When the whirlwind came, the seas closed over Ulysses and the other voyagers. The "other pole" Ulysses sees in his tale is usually identified with the Mountain of Purgatory, which Dante will ascend in the next poem. The connection being that Ulysses died in the shadow of a "mountain" just as he is in Hell.

Canto XXVI

Study Questions

1. Dante begins Canto XXVI with irony. Describe this irony.
2. How are the Counselors of Fraud punished?
3. What does Virgil think of Dante's desire to speak to the flame?
4. Does Dante get to ask his questions?
5. Who is the flame who tells them of his travels?
6. What was the Palladium?
7. How was Eteocles killed?
8. What was unusual about the funeral pyre of Eteocles and his brother?
9. How was Ulysses killed?
10. What is the name of Deidamia's son?

Answers

1. Dante says for Florence to rejoice because it is so well known—in Hell.
2. The Counselors of Fraud are punished by the fire burning above their heads, through which they must speak.
3. Virgil thinks that Dante's wish is worthy of high praise and in no way wrong.
4. Virgil reads Dante's thoughts and asks the questions for Dante.
5. The flame who tells them of his travels is Ulysses.
6. The Palladium was the statue of Troy, on which the safety of the city was to depend.
7. Eteocles and his brother killed each other in battle.
8. After their death, Eteocles's and his brother's bodies were placed on a funeral pyre; the flames stayed separate and would not united even in death.

9. Ulysses and his crew were drowned when the seas closed over them.
10. Deidamia's son is named Achilles.

Suggested Essay Topics
1. Why did Virgil not want Dante to speak to the flames?
2. Ancients used fire to purify water, food, and even utensils. Is there any relation to the purifying power of fire and the counselors' speaking through a flame? Explain.

Canto XXVII

New Character:

Guido da Montefeltro: *Ghibelline leader who persuaded Pope Boniface VIII to use treachery to gain the fortress of Palestrina*

Summary

The flame moves on when Virgil dismisses it.

Another flame speaks. Dante compares the speaking voice of this flame to the voice coming from a metal bull which was used to roast victims alive. The voice asks for news from earth.

Virgil gives Dante the right to answer. Dante says that there is no strife in Romagna; that Ravenna and Cervia have the same ruler; that another city is governed by the Green Claw; and that Cesena is suffering from misrule by its leaders.

Dante asks that the flame now tell him who he is. The flame says that he will tell the truth since he does not believe that Dante will be able to return to the earth. The shade says that he was a soldier and then a friar; the High Priest, however, forced him to go back into the mesh of battle. The Priest asked the shade to tell him how to defeat Palestrina and promised that the shade would be absolved. The shade died before he had been contrite; uncontrite is unabsolved. The shade found himself in Hell for counseling fraud.

Canto XXVII

The two travelers see that those who cause division in life receive their own merchandise in death.

Analysis

Another flame asks Dante for information of the world. In the day of Phalaris, the ruler of Sicily, Perillus had made a brass bull to roast people alive. The ruler made Perillus the first victim. Dante compares the voice of this flame to the voice from the bull.

Virgil allows Dante to speak and tell the shade of news from earth. Dante uses symbolism to indicate that Sinibaldo degli Ordelaffi rules Forli; that a father and son (Malatesta and Malatestino), who were Black Guelphs of Romini, rule Montagna; that Mainardo Pagano rules both Lamone and Santerno and tries to behave like a Ghibelline and a Guelph; and that the leaders of Cesean misrule the town.

The shade gives information about himself to Dante only because he does not believe that Dante will leave the pit. The shade is a great Ghibelline leader by the name of Guido da Montefeltro. Using Guido to transmit deceptive advice, Pope Boniface VIII conspired against the Colonna family in warfare in 1297. The Colonna family had robbed the Papal treasury and retired to Palestrina. The Pope declared that the Colonnas would have full amnesty upon surrender, but they broke this promise. Upon rebelling again, the Colonnas were excommunicated. In 1303 Boniface himself became a prisoner.

Dante and Virgil see the sinners receive their "merchandise" as they travel.

Study Questions

1. For what does the tall flame have to wait before it can pass on to another place?
2. What was the purpose of the Sicilian bull?
3. What is meant by the statement that uncontrite is unabsolved?
4. What is the occupation of the shade before he became a friar?
5. Who is the shade who asks of conditions on earth in this canto?

6. Why does the shade reveal his identity to Dante?
7. What does Dante tell him of the condition of Romagna?
8. Why is the shade present in Bowge VIII?
9. The shade says it was brought to Minos. Who is Minos?
10. Why had Constantine sought Silvester, according to the shade?

Answers

1. The tall flame has to wait for Virgil's permission before it can pass on to another place.
2. The Sicilian bull was used to roast its victims alive.
3. If one is *not sorry* (uncontrite), one is *not forgiven* (unabsolved).
4. Before the habit, the shade was a man of arms, a soldier, a Cordelier.
5. The shade is a great Ghibelline leader by the name of Guido da Montefeltro.
6. The shade reveals his identity to Dante because he does not believe that Dante will return to earth.
7. Romagna, Dante tells him, has no open strife at the time, but there is always feuding in the area.
8. The shade had counseled fraud.
9. Minos is the judge in the underworld.
10. According to the shade, Constantine had sought Silvester to cure his leprosy. Silvester did this through baptism.

Suggested Essay Topics

1. Explain how Guido da Montefeltro became a resident of Hell and particularly a resident of the particular Circle VIII, Bowge VIII.
2. Dante gives, in effect, a news update to the shade in Circle VIII. What news might he report if he were making his trip in the current year?

Canto XXVIII

New Characters:

Sowers of Discord: *Created discord on earth; their bodies are torn apart in Hell*

Mahomet: *Founder of Islam (Mohammed)*

Pier da Medicina: *Incited civil strife; disseminated scandal and misrepresentation; incited feuds between two Romagna families*

Curio: *Brought about civil strife; tongue removed for punishment*

Mosca: *Brought Florentine division by creating Guelphs and Ghibellines*

Bertrand de Born: *Headless shade who helped increase feud between Henry II of England and his young son Prince Henry*

Summary

Dante is appalled at the suffering he sees from the bridge over the Ninth Bowge. He tries, in vain, to verbalize the extent of the pain by comparing it to battles, deaths, and wounds which the readers may recognize.

The two travelers see the Sowers of Discord in the Ninth Trench. The punishment of these shades is that a fiend rends their bodies in two with a sharp sword; the sinners can even rend their own bodies in two pieces.

The two poets are addressed by Mahomet, the founder of Islam, who states that Ali walks in the pit before him. He refers to places (like the plains between Vercelli and Marcabo, the passage near La Cattolica) and people (like Guido and Angiolello of Fano; the men of Argo; and Mosca). Mahomet shows the poets Curio, now with a missing tongue.

Dante sees an amazing sight: a body without a head and a hand carrying the head by the hair. When the figure approaches the two poets, it places the head on its shoulders so that it can speak. The two learn that the shade is Bertrand de Born.

Analysis

To emphasize the bloodshed and injury in Hell, Dante uses a particular literary device: he says that tongues are unable to describe the sights; this same device is used in Canto XXV.

Dante makes reference to Apulia's ground, which is a place in southeast Italy where many wars and battles occurred. According to Livy (a Roman historian of the years 57 B.C. to A.D. 17), the seacoast town of Troy in Asia Minor was taken by the Greeks to recover Helen. Dante mentions the battles against Robert Guiscard, who himself had fought against the Greeks. and the place of Ceperano, where the barons of Apulia had deserted and Charles of Anjou had entered and defeated Manfred in 1266 at Benevento. Dante also alludes to the field of Tagliacozzo, where Charles of Anjou defeated Manfred's nephew by allowing Alard de Valery to advise his army to retreat. When the "winning" army came searching for plunder, the retreating army returned and won the battle.

Mahomet (an Italian spelling for Mohammed, the founder of Islam) had brought division to the Christians by setting up his own sect. Ali is a reference to the nephew of Mahomet who brought division to the followers of Mahomet by setting up his own sect within.

This canto mentions several places. Two such places are the town Lombardy, with Vercelli at its western edge. Marcabo is a castle at the eastern extremity of Lombardy. The passage near La Cattolica is a reference to a town in Italy on the Adriatic Sea.

Canto XXVIII mentions several people. Guido dei Cavalcanti had been Dante's friend and, like Angiolello da Calignano, was from Fano. Mosca had been partly responsible for the conflict between the Guelphs and Ghibellines in Florence. When Buondelmonte dei Buondelmonti was accused of jilting his betrothed, the townspeople decided how to settle the quarrel. Mosca dei Lamberti made a comment to suggest stoning the man to death, and the result was the murder of Buondelmonte. The entire city became involved in the rivalry between families and political parties. Mosca is an example of one guilty of creating family discord.

Curio (Caius Scribonius Curio) was an adherent of Pompey and had been brought to Rome by Julius Caesar. When Rome declared

Canto XXVIII

Caesar an enemy of Rome, Curio advised Caesar to cross the Rubicon and march upon Rome. Trial proceedings found Curio guilty of creating civil discord.

Bertrand de Born, the headless shade, helped to increase the feud between Henry II of England and his young son, Prince Henry. The symbolism of a head minus a body suggests the pain of a father minus a son; King David in the Old Testament experienced this same pain without his son Absalom. Bertrand de Born is an example of family discord.

Study Questions

1. What is the punishment of the Sowers of Discord?
2. Who is Absalom?
3. Who is Bertrand de Born?
4. Why does Virgil say that Dante is in Hell?
5. What advice does the outcast give to Caesar?
6. What is the outcast's punishment for giving ill advice to Caesar and for creating discord?
7. How is the outcast able to speak?
8. Which type of discord does Bertrand represent?
9. Which type of discord does Mahomet represent?
10. Which type of discord does Curio represent?

Answers

1. The Sowers of Discord received bodily injury specific to their crimes for their actions.
2. Absalom was David's son; David was King of Israel.
3. Bertrand de Born is the shade with his head in his hand. He is guilty of starting the quarrel between Henry II and his son.
4. Virgil says that Dante is in Hell to find "full experience of the Way."
5. The outcast told Caesar that delays were dangerous and he gives the sign for the civil strife to start.

6. The outcast had his tongue cut from his mouth because of the ill advice he had given to Caesar and for having created discord.

7. The outcast is able to speak because he puts his head on his body.

8. Bertrand is guilty of having created family discord.

9. Mahomet is guilty of having created religious discord.

10. Curio is guilty of having created civil discord.

Suggested Essay Topics

1. Is there a relationship between the punishment of the Sowers of Discord and their sins? Explain your answer.

2. Describe the type(s) of conflict that is(are) present in Canto XXVIII. Give examples of each. (Some types of conflict might include person-against-person conflict, person-against-self conflict, person-against-society conflict, and person-against-nature conflict.)

Canto XXIX

New Characters:

Falsifiers: *Punished in the Ninth Trench; victims of disease and illness*

Capocchio: *Student with Dante; an alchemist who called self an "ape of nature" because of his power to mimic or to produce a draught*

Aretine: *Griffolino d'Arezza; a physicist; took money for promising miracles; burned at stake for falsifying*

Summary

Dante spends some time watching the people in the Ninth Bowge because he expects to see one of his kinsman, Geri del Bello; Virgil urges Dante to continue the trip immediately and think of other things. Virgil indicates that he saw Geri del Bello while Dante

Canto XXIX

was watching one who lived in Altaforte. Dante explains that Geri had been killed and his death was still unavenged. Virgil and Dante note that disease is rampant in the trench. Dante compares it with Valdichiana, Maremma, and Sardinia. The pit contains the falsifiers. Dante says that no sadder sight was seen even in Aegina.

One of the shades in the Bowge X identifies himself as Aretine, who was burned at the stake because of Albero of Siena. Aretine had said he could fly; such falsification, along with his work as an alchemist, brought his execution since Albero told of being cheated by Aretine.

Capocchio, who could produce a drought and had been a fellow student with Dante, identified himself after mentioning four others: Stricca, Niccolo, Caccia d'Ascian, and Abbagliato.

Analysis

Virgil says that while Dante was observing the person from Altaforte (Bertrand de Born), the kinsman passed by without speaking. Dante believes that his kinsman ignored him because his murder is still unavenged.

Dante and Virgil see physically ill people lying in the trench. Dante compares the trench to Valdichiana and Maremma (areas of swamp in Tuscany) and to Sardinia (another unhealthy area known for malaria).

Aegina was an area where the god Juno sent a pestilence to remove all the people. To repopulate the aea, Jupiter turned ants into people.

Study Questions

1. Why does Dante spend time observing the people in the Ninth Trench?
2. What does Virgil say that his business is in Hell?
3. Why is Aretine being punished in Hell?
4. What is the punishment for falsifying?
5. How large is the fosse, according to Canto XXIX?
6. According to the myth, how did Jupiter repopulate the island of Aegina?

7. According to the myth, why did Jupiter have to repopulate the island of Aegina?
8. What was the "joke" that Aretine had told Albero of Siena?
9. How did Albero punish Aretine?
10. What are some examples of falsifying?

Answers
1. Dante spends time observing the people in the Ninth Trench because he is looking for a kinsman.
2. Virgil says that his business in Hell is to show Dante what Hell is like.
3. Aretine is being punished for the crime of alchemy.
4. The sin of falsifying is punished by disease.
5. The fosse is 22 miles round.
6. Jupiter repopulated the island of Aegina with ants.
7. Jupiter had to repopulate the island of Aegina because Juno had sent pestilence which destroyed the people of the island of Aegina.
8. The "joke" that Aretine had told to Albero of Siena was that he could take wings and could fly.
9. Aretine punished Albero by burning him.
10. Some examples of falsifying include alchemy, making shoddy products, consenting to dishonesty, the sale of the church, tampering with things to be sold, and the sale of sexual relationships.

Suggested Essay Topics
1. Describe the sights in the Ninth Circle. How does the punishment in the Ninth Circle relate to the sin of falsifying?
2. The harlot in Canto XVIII and the two shades in Canto XXIX both use their nails. Compare and contrast this use of nails for the harlot and the shades.

Canto XXX

New Characters:

Gianni Schicchi: *Falsifier who dressed as Buoso and dictated a new will*

Myrrha: *According to Ovid, disguised self and was impregnated by own father (King of Cyprus); turned into a myrtle tree and bore Adonis—a son—through the bark*

Master Adam: *Counterfeited Romena coins bearing John the Baptist*

Guido, Alexander, and their Brother: *Blamed for Adam's counterfeiting; part of the Conti Guidi family*

Sinon of Troy: *Greek spy who persuaded the Trojans to bring the wooden horse into the gates of Troy*

The False Wife: *Reference to the wife of Potiphar (Book of Genesis); tries to lie with Joseph and, when he refuses, falsely accuses him*

Summary

Dante begins Canto XXX with examples of fury from mythology. First, he identifies Jupiter and his obsession for Semele, which brought about Juno's vengeance upon the Thebans. Juno caused Athamas, the brother-in-law of Semele, to undergo a fierce madness which resulted in Athamas's killing his baby. Athamas's wife drowned herself and her other child.

Dante recalls how Hecuba, the wife of the King of Troy, saw her daughter slain, found her son dead by the sea, and, while a captive herself, became insane. Dante remarks that none of this fury compares with what he sees from two shades in the Eighth Circle.

One shade falls on Capocchio—Dante's former friend and fellow student. The Aretine tells Dante that the shade is Gianni Schicchi, who had at one time dressed as Buoso and dictated a new will. The Aretine also recognizes another shade, which he introduces to Dante as Myrrha. Myrrha had disguised herself and had gone to her own father to do a shameful act.

Dante sees a diseased shade with dropsy and a puffed body. This body identifies himself as Master Adam, who in Romena had counterfeited coins bearing the image of John the Baptist. Adam states that Guido, Alexander, and their brother—all counts at Romena—had caused him to commit the false act.

Dante asks who the shades are that he can see close by; Adam explains that one is Sinon of Troy and one is the false wife who accused Joseph unjustly.

Before Dante's eyes, Sinon and Adam begin to quarrel and fight. Dante watches agog until Virgil threatens to quarrel with Dante if he continues to gape. Dante is shamed, but Virgil tells him to think no more of it; Virgil concludes by gently reminding Dante that to watch such a display is a vulgar thing to do.

Analysis

Canto XXX is filled with conflict. Dante sets the stage for the conflict that is to come by recalling rage and fury depicted in mythology and saying that none of it compares with what he sees in Hell—particularly in the Eighth Circle.

After Capocchio is dragged by one of the two shades, the Aretine (Griffolino) is left trembling. He explains that the shades are Gianni Schicchi and Myrrha, who had seduced her father the King of Cyprus. When the King of Cyprus recognized his daughter Myrrha and tried to kill her, she fled and turned into a myrtle tree; her child was Adonis who came from her trunk.

Guido, Alexander, and their brother are references to the Conti Guidi family. Adam implies that one of the Conti family is currently in Hell.

Sinon of Troy is the Greek spy who persuaded the Trojans to bring the wooden horse into the gates of Troy. The false wife is an allusion to the wife of Potiphar in the Book of Genesis. When she tries to lie with Joseph and he refuses her, she falsely accuses him anyway.

Virgil chides Dante for watching a display of anger between Adam and Sinon. When Dante takes the admonition very seriously, Virgil tells him not to overreact. Virgil does remind Dante that watching such a display is a low, base, vulgar thing to do.

Canto XXX

Study Questions
1. What is Dante doing when Virgil reprimands him?
2. What is Dante's reaction to Virgil's reprimand?
3. What images of falsifiers are found in Bowge X?
4. In Canto XXX about what does the Greek lie?
5. Whose image is on the counterfeit coins in Canto XXX?
6. How did Hecuba kill herself?
7. What is the sin of Myrrha?
8. What is the sin of Gianni Schicchi?
9. Who is Capocchio?
10. What did Juno send to Athamas for revenge?

Answers
1. Dante is watching the sinners and listening intently to what they say when Virgil reprimanded him.
2. Virgil's reprimand of Dante brings Dante shame.
3. In Bowge X are falsifiers of person, of words, and of money.
4. The Greek that Dante describes in Canto XXX had lied about the wooden horse that the Greeks used to hide soldiers when they took the horse into the walls of Troy.
5. In Canto XXX the image of John the Baptist is on the counterfeit coins.
6. Hecuba killed herself by drowning.
7. Myrrha's sin was that she lay with her own father.
8. Schicchi's sin was that he dressed as another and dictated a will.
9. Capocchio had been the student-friend of Dante.
10. Juno sent madness to Athamas for revenge.

Suggested Essay Topics

1. Explain the scene that Dante is observing when Virgil criticizes him. Why does Virgil criticize Dante for observing?
2. Two women—the false wife and Myrrha—are in Circle Eight. Women are not described in detail in most of the other circles. What are the sins of these women? Why do you think Dante does not describe women in the other circles? How do you think their absence in the other circles and their presence in this circle affects the reader's image of women?

Canto XXXI

New Characters:

The Giants: *Visible from the waist up above the rim of the well; include Nimrod (who loosed the bands of common speech), Ephialtes (who attacked Jove), and Antaeus (who is invincible on earth but not in the air or sky; carries Virgil and Dante to the pit bottom)*

Summary

Dante speaks of Virgil's tongue which had wounded him but now salves his wounds. As Dante and Virgil continue on their journey, they hear the clamor of those below them. Dante sees some towers and asks what they might be. Virgil says that the fog has changed Dante's vision and kindly tells Dante that the pillars are giants set in a ring and hidden from the navel down. Dante says that the decision of nature to discontinue the making of these giants was a good one; he says that a thinking mind combined with strength and malice would give a combination against which people of a regular size would not be able to protect themselves.

From the place on the giant where the mantle is buckled downward to the ground is a full 30 hands.

Dante hears one of the giants begin to howl in a garbled tongue. Virgil commands the giant to use his horn and not his tongue; Virgil tells Dante that the giant is Nimrod, who caused the world's many languages to appear.

Canto XXXI

The next giant that Dante sees is Ephialtes, who had fought against Jove. Dante sees that he is in chains and Virgil explains that this is punishment for the giant's aggression. Virgil informs Dante that Antaeus will carry them to the bottom of sin.

Virgil addresses Antaeus as the one who came from the vale where Scipio made Hannibal turn tail. Virgil asks Antaeus not to make them go to Typhon or Tityus but to perform the duty for them. Dante looks at Antaeus and compares the experience to gazing at Carisenda. Antaeus easily picks them up for the journey.

Analysis

Canto XXXI contains many examples of conflict. Dante begins Canto XXXI by commenting on the correction given him by Virgil (person-against-person conflict) and how the conflict is resolved by Virgil himself. Dante feels terror and struggles to control himself during this period (person-against-self-conflict).

The giant creatures that they see in this area, Dante comments, no longer increase. Dante sees this decision as a good decision because neither the shades of a regular size nor the people of the earth are able to protect themselves against these creatures because of their great size. From the place the mantle (cloak) buckles (the shoulder) down is 30 hands. The comparison to hands is significant. Measurement in hands is usually confined to animals, like the horse, and not to humans; this reflects the size of the giants and relegates them a status lower than humans.

The garbled language of the giant Nimrod is a reference to the Tower of Babel, the source of the many languages on the face of the earth according to Genesis. Antaeus is the giant which will carry them to the bottom of sin; Antaeus is a giant which had been invincible as long as he stayed in contact with the earth.

Virgil addresses Antaeus. The vale to which Virgil refers is the vale where Scipio fought against Hannibal and caused Hannibal to retreat; the valley is called the Valley of Bagrada near Zama. Virgil requests that Antaeus carry them to the bottom of sin and not to make it necessary for them to request the favor of the giants Typhon and Tityus. When Dante looks up at the giant, he describes the experience as similar to that of looking at a tower called Carisenda; this structure gave viewers the feeling that the tower was leaning toward them if they looked upward at it. Dante felt that the giant was looking toward him as Dante gazed upward at the giant.

Study Questions
1. What does Virgil say causes Dante not to see well?
2. What are the towers that Dante thinks he sees?
3. What does Dante think about nature's decision to discontinue the giants?
4. How large (using the measurement of hands) is the giant from the place where the mantle is buckled to the ground?
5. Who is Ephialtes?
6. What is the punishment of Ephialtes?
7. Who is Nimrod?
8. What is the duty of Antaeus?
9. Who is the military leader that Scipio causes to retreat?
10. What is Carisenda?

Answers
1. Virgil says that the fog has caused Dante not to see well.
2. The towers that Dante thinks he sees are actually giants.
3. Dante says that nature's decision to discontinue the giants is a wise one because persons of regular size cannot protect themselves against such large creatures, which also have some intelligence.
4. From the place where the giant's mantle is buckled downward in hands is a full 30 hands.
5. Ephialtes is the giant who had fought against Jove.
6. The punishment of Ephialtes is that he remain in chains because of his attack on Jove.
7. Nimrod is the giant who is responsible for the many languages on the earth.

8. Antaeus is the giant who will carry them to the bottom of sin.
9. Scipio causes Hannibal to retreat in battle.
10. Carisenda is a tower that gives viewers the feeling that it is leaning toward them if they look upward at it.

Suggested Essay Topics
1. Discuss the conflicts found in Canto XXXI.
2. Why do you think the giants are condemned to Hell?

Canto XXXII

New Characters:

Napoleone and Alexandro degli Alberto: *Two shades in Region i, Circle IX; brothers; slew one another in fight over family land*

Sassol Mascheroni: *In Region i, Circle IX; murdered uncle's only son (Sassol's cousin) and took the inheritance.*

Camicion de' Pazzi: *Introduced shades to Dante in Region i, Circle IX; quick to identify other wrong-doers; less-likely to identify own wrongs; murdered Ubertino, his own kinsman*

Summary

Dante has doubts about his ability to describe with words what he has seen in Hell. A new sight reaches his eyes in Region i of Circle IX. He sees a river, the river Cocytus, frozen solid and remarks that even the Danube in Austria could not freeze as solidly. Dante predicts that even if high mountains crashed upon it, the ice would not break under their weight.

Dante sees shades in the cold and notes that their tears are frozen. One shade explains to him that the two which seem inseparable are Napoleone and Alexandro degli Alberto, whose father once controlled the valley. The chatty shade tells Dante that one of those near him is Sassol Mascheroni.

Only after identifying others does the shade tell Dante about himself.

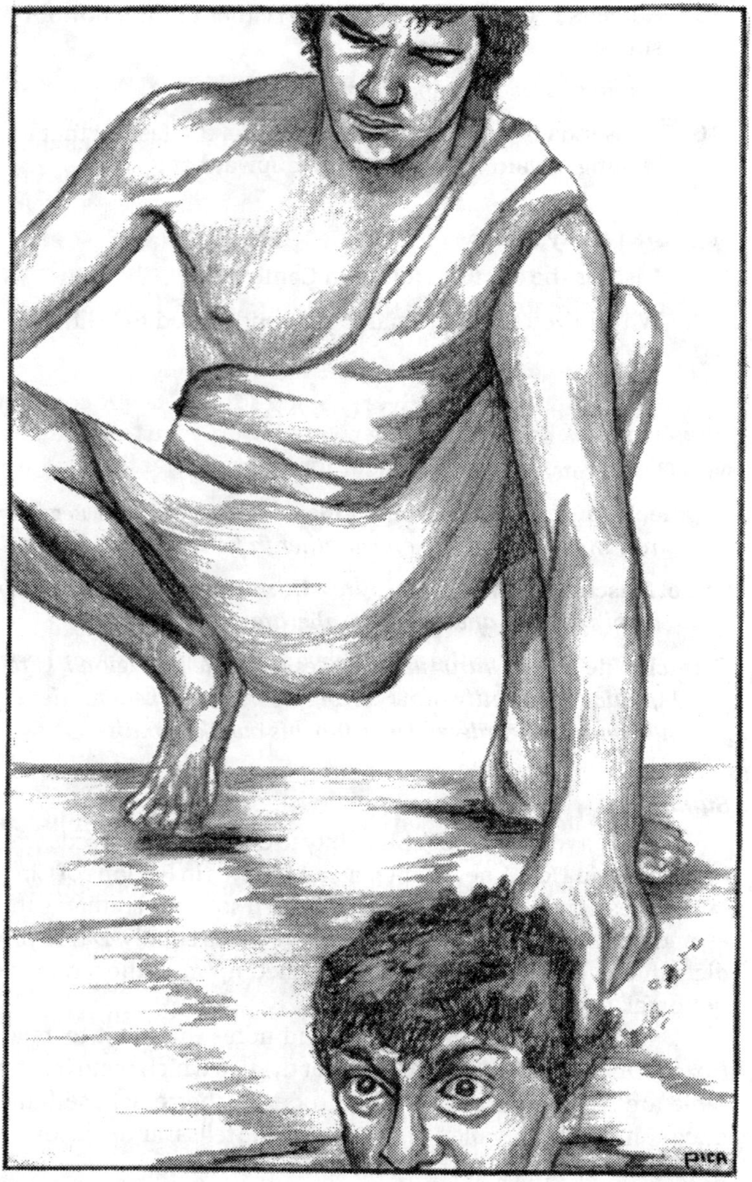

Canto XXXII

The shade is Camicion de' Pazzi. He is waiting for Carlin to "make excuses" for Camicion. Dante sees the faces of the shades in the frozen water. One of the shades begins to curse. Dante asks why he is cursing and the shade asks why Dante is going about kicking the faces of the shades in Region ii, Antenora. Dante becomes angry and demands to know the name of the shade; Dante even begins pulling the shade's hair. About this time another shade addresses Dante's victim as "Bocca." Dante also recognizes Duera; the shades tell him that other traitors to their country are here; these traitors include Beccaria, Gianni de' Soldanier, Ganelon, and Tibbald.

Dante sees a man gnawing the head of one shade near him and chewing the part where brain meets the bone. Dante compares the shade's zeal in eating another with that of Tydeus as he gnawed Menalippus. Dante asks the shade for the reason for his condition.

Analysis

The cold region of Caina (named from Cain who kills his brother Abel in Genesis) causes much suffering to those in the pit. Dante observes personally the suffering of those sentenced to remain there. It contains those who have acted violently towards their own family.

One shade identifies Napoleone and Alexandro degli Alberto, two brothers who had slain one another in a fight over family land and are, therefore, traitors to their kindred. Sassol Mascheroni is another inhabitant identified by the chatty shade; Sassol murdered his uncle's only son (Sassol's cousin) and took the inheritance.

Camicion de' Pazzi is quick to identify other wrong-doers. He is less-likely to identify his own wrongs. Camicion murdered Ubertino, his own kinsman. Camicion alludes to the fact that his errors will not seem so bad when Carlin arrives. Carlino dei Pazzi—one of Camicion's kin—was bribed by the Blacks to surrender the castle he was holding for the Whites; he later sold it to the Whites again.

The shade who is giving Dante all this information refuses to reveal his own name, but another sinner addresses him as "Bocca." Bocca is Bocca degli Abati, a Ghibelline. In the Battle of Montaperti, he had fought on the Guelph side; during this battle he cut off the hand of the man who carried the standard. The Florentine soldiers went into a panic when they saw the flag fall, and they lost the battle.

Dante also recognizes Duera; Duera is Buoso da Duera, a commander of the Ghibellines. Duera had sold a passage to the opposing French army and was, therefore, a traitor to his country.

Gianni de' Soldanier had supposedly been a Ghibelline, but when the Guelphs rebelled, he led the Guelphs. Ganelon was the father-in-law of Roland, the nephew of Charlemagne; Ganelon had betrayed the army of Charlemagne to the enemy, who killed Roland. Tibbald had opened the gates of Faenza to the enemy, the Guelphs. Tesauro dei Beccaria had lost his head for accusations that he plotted with the Ghibellines against the Guelphs.

Tydeus was the king of Calydon; he was one of the Seven against Thebes. Menalippus mortally wounded Tydeus; however, Tydeus still managed to kill Menalippus, to gnaw the scalp and to tear out the brains of his enemy.

Study Questions

1. What is the temperature like in Region ii?
2. What does Dante find in the lake beneath him?
3. What is Region ii called?
4. In Canto XXXII what is one of the shades eating that causes Dante horror?
5. One of the shades would not tell his name. How is Dante able to learn his name?
6. What is unusual about the tears of the shades in Region i?
7. Whose sin is more severe: traitors to country or traitors to kin?
8. What about the location of that sin in Hell enables one to know the answer to question 7?
9. Where does the land of Caina get its name?
10. Bocca tells Dante the names of others in the region. What does this tell you about Bocca's repentance?

Answers

1. The temperature in Region ii is extremely cold.
2. Dante finds the heads and faces of shades in the lake beneath him.
3. Region ii is called Antenora.
4. One of the shades in the region is eating the man beside him.
5. Another shade calls the name of the shade unknown to Dante and Dante is able to learn the shade's name.
6. The tears of the shades in Region i are frozen.
7. The sin of being unfaithful to one's kin is not as severe as the sin of being unfaithful to one's country.
8. One would know that being unfaithful to one's country is more severe than being unfaithful to one's kin since the prior sin is located lower in Hell.
9. The land of Caina gets its name from Cain, who killed his brother Abel; their story is in Genesis.
10. Bocca has not repented of his sin of being a traitor; he continues to betray those who are here in Hell by revealing their name.

Suggested Essay Topics

1. The traitors to their kindred are confined to Region i, where it is cold. How does this punishment fit the crime they committed? Explain your answer.
2. Why do you think that there are no women in this region? Explain your answer.

Canto XXXIII

New Characters:

Count Ugolino della Gherardesca: *Guelph leader who ate human flesh; imprisoned in the Tower of Famine; saw sons and grandsons starve*

Archbishop Ruggieri degli Ubaldini: *Imprisoned Count Ugolino*
Friar Alberigo: *Soul in Patolomaea, where traitors to their guests reside*
Ser Branca d' Oria: *Shade in Patolomaea responsible for murder*

Summary

The shade who had eaten of the body of another person begins to speak to Dante. He tells Dante that he is Count Ugolino and that his victim is Archbishop Roger. In life he had trusted Roger, but Roger had betrayed him.

(An explanation of the above helps the reader to understand the summary. Count Ugolino della Gherardesca and his grandson Nino Dei Visconti headed two rival, powerful Guelph parties in 1288. Ugolino turned traitor and joined ranks with the Archbishop Ruggieri degli Ubaldini. As soon as the Archbishop and his forces were able to drive Nino out, however, the Archbishop turned on Ugolino. The Guelphs placed Ugolino and four of his sons and grandsons in a tower, which the people later called "the Tower of Famine." The Archbishop ordered the key to be thrown in the river and the prisoners were isolated. After eight days the tower was opened and all the occupants were dead.)

In the canto, the shade tells Dante that one night he saw Roger with his hounds chasing a wolf and its young. In the morning the Count's children cried for food, but the Count listened to their tears as one made of stone. He heard his little Anselm ask what was to become of them. Time passed and still they had no food. The Count gnawed at his own hands in pain for his children. They, who thought he was hungry, begged him to eat them rather than himself. On the fourth day Gaddo died. Later Il Brigata, Hugh, and Anselm died. By the sixth day the Count was blind; later he died also from famine.

As the two poets move through this icy region, they hear the voice of one crying out to them. Dante says that he will help that one if the one crying will tell them his name. The crying shade says he is Friar Alberigo. He says that his soul is in Ptolomaea, but his body is elsewhere. The Friar speculates that when his soul was separated from his body by the shears of Atropos, it fell to Region iii of

Canto XXXIII

Circle IX; this region is called Ptolomaea. He says also that the body is occupied by a fiend who will remain there until its years are up. The Friar says that the shade wintering here until the years of his body are up is Ser Branca d' Oria. The shade asks Dante to open his frozen eyes for him, but Dante does not.

Analysis

The wolf and its young are symbolic of Ugolino and his sons and grandsons, even though the four "young" victims were actually not children. The four victims were 1) Nino, the Count's grandson, who was also known as Il Brigata; 2) the Count's grandson Anselm; 3) the Count's son Gaddo; and 4) his son Hugh. The four were young men, not mere children.

The mention of moving Gorgona and Caprara from the River Arno are references to moving two islands from the water; these islands belonged to Pisans. Their conquest by the Florentine army involved giving them to the Florentine army.

The two poets pass into the new region of Ptolomaea, where reside the Traitors to Guests. Dante promises to help one shade who cries out if the shade will reveal his identity. The shade gives his name as Friar Alberigo. This man had argued with his brother Manfred. After Manfred became angry and struck Alberigo in the face, Alberigo professed to have forgiven his brother. Alberigo invited his brother to his home; armed people are offered to attack and kill Manfred when Alberigo shouts, "Bring on the fruit!" Alberigo is a traitor to his guests and, therefore, resides in Ptolomaea. Particular to Ptolomaea, a man may be brought there still alive with his body inhabited by a demon.

Ser Branca d' Oria is a Ghibelline who invited his father-in-law Michael Zanche (mentioned in Canto XXII) to a dinner party. At the dinner party Zanche is killed.

The shade asks Dante to undo his eyes, but Dante does not do so for the same reason mentioned in Canto VIII: Dante is accepting the judgment of God and is placing himself on God's side.

Study Questions

1. Why does the sinner speak to explain his ugly feast?
2. Which of the shades is Count Ugolino?
3. What is the occupation of the shade who is being eaten?
4. How had Count Ugolino died?
5. What relation to Count Ugolino were the four who died, according to the canto?
6. What is the day when Dante visits the lowest area of Hell?
7. What promise does Dante fail to keep?
8. What was the dreadful den in which Ugolino died?
9. What is the name given the dreadful den after Ugolino was found?
10. Who was Anselm?

Answers

1. The sinner tells his story to shame the one who had sinned against him.
2. Count Ugolino is the shade who was feasting on the head of the other.
3. The shade who was being eaten was an archbishop.
4. Count Ugolino had died of famine.
5. The four who died with Count Ugolino were his sons, according to the canto.
6. The day on which Dante visits the lowest realms of Hell is Saturday.
7. Dante refuses to open the eyes of the shade.
8. Ugolino's dreadful den is a tower.
9. The dreadful tower, or den, is called the Tower of Famine after Count Ugolino and his sons were found dead.
10. Anselm was the youngest son of Count Ugolino in the canto; in life he was the grandson.

Suggested Essay Topics
1. Dante promises to remove the ice from the shade's eyes, but he does not. Why does Dante break his promise?
2. What conflicts does Dante include in Canto XXXIII?

Canto XXXIV

New Characters:

Dis (Satan): *Ruler of the pit*

Judas Iscariot: *Resident of Region iv of Dis; betrayer of Jesus*

Brutus: *Later a Shakespearean character; opposed to the Divine and secular world; a resident of Dis*

Cassius: *Defeated by Anthony and took his own life; later a Shakespearean character; a resident of Dis*

Summary

Canto XXXIV begins with the statement that "The banners of the King of Hell go forth." Virgil asks Dante if it will be possible for Dante to recognize Dis (Satan) if they see him. The two pass over Judecca.

Dante sees Satan in Region iv, Dis. Satan is devouring Judas Iscariot. Cassius and Brutus are also residents of this lowest region.

The two poets climb down—and then up—the body of Satan. At the end of the journey they can see the stars once more.

Analysis

The two poets pass over the region of Judecca, the last ring of the circle; this region is that in which the traitors to their Lords reside. The traitors here are totally covered with ice.

Symbolism is used in the description of Satan. His colors refer to the colors of people all over the world. If Lucifer's present ugliness is equivalent to his earlier beauty before his desert, his betrayal must have been monstrous to have created such hideousness.

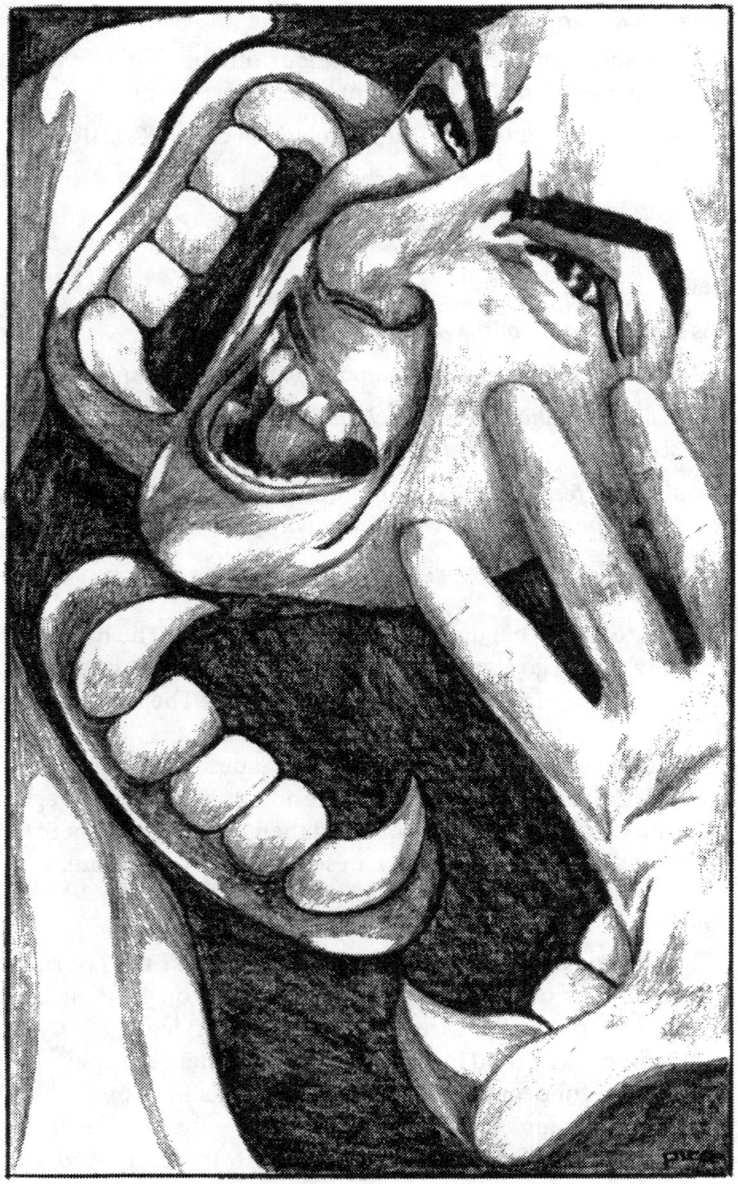
pico

Canto XXXIV

Judas is the first shade that they see in Dis. He is suffering severe pain because of his sins against God. Judas opposed God and is here for that reason. The other two shades that they recognize are Cassius and Brutus. They are here because of their opposition to both secular and divine world. The stronger ones—God and His son—banish him to the lower region. Other dark angels go with him to this lower place.

The body of Satan is between 1,500 and 1,800 feet tall; the two poets use his hair and body to cling to as they make their trip downward; when they reach the center (the navel) of the giant (Dis), Dante and Virgil begin their upward climb.

The canto ends with the hopefulness of upward motion as well as the word *stars* as they once again see the night sky.

Study Questions

1. Why does Dante not describe all the sights he sees in Canto XXXIV?
2. What name does Dante give Satan in Canto XXXIV?
3. How does Satan's size compare with that of the giants?
4. How are Dante and Virgil able to climb out of the pit?
5. What is the sin of Iscariot?
6. What is Satan doing to the sinners in Region iv?
7. What is the name of Region iv?
8. Name one of the shades that Satan is devouring.
9. Dante says that he grasps the hair of the Worm. To what is he referring?
10. Dante refers to Lucifer in Canto XXXIV. Who is Lucifer?

Answers

1. Dante does not have the words to describe all the sights he sees in Canto XXXIV.
2. Dante calls Satan Dis in Canto XXXIV.
3. Satan is taller than the giants; they come only to his armpits.

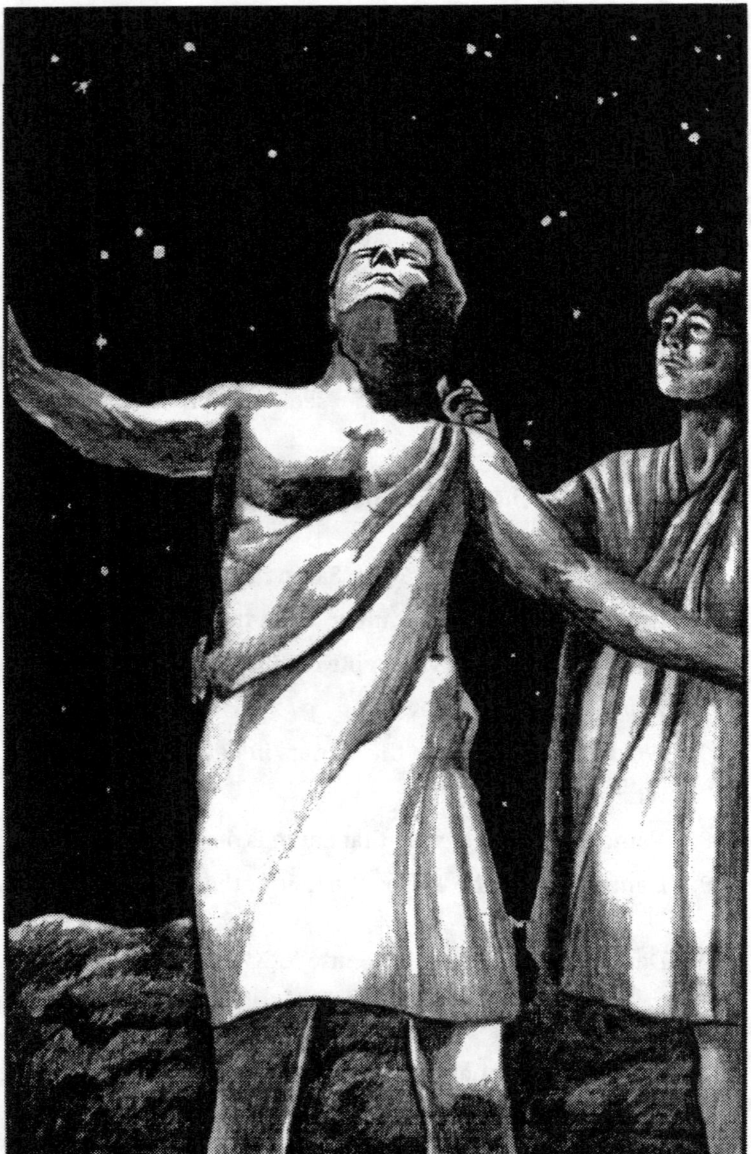

Canto XXXIV

4. Dante and Virgil are able to climb out of the pit by climbing up Satan's body.
5. Iscariot had betrayed Jesus, his Lord.
6. Satan is devouring the sinners in Region iv.
7. The name of Region iv is Judecca.
8. The shades that Satan is devouring are Cassius, Brutus, and Judas.
9. The hair of the Worm is a reference to the body of Satan.
10. Lucifer is another name for Satan.

Suggested Essay Topics

1. Describe Dis (Satan) as he appears in Canto XXXIV.
2. What do you think is the symbolism of Dante's leaving Hell on Easter Sunday? Explain your answer.

SECTION THREE

Sample Analytical Paper Topics

The following paper topics should test your understanding of the work as a whole and allow you to analyze important themes and literary devices. Following each question is a sample outline to get you started.

Topic #1

There are three main themes in traditional literature; these themes include the picaresque theme, in which the character travels or makes a journey; the reversal of fortune theme, in which the character has his or her situation in life changed; and the survival of the unfittest theme, in which a character who is not really equipped for survival is able to endure.

Which of these themes apply/applies to Dante's *Inferno*?

Outline

I. Thesis Statement: *All three of the main themes in traditional literature apply to Dante's* Inferno; *these themes include the picaresque theme, the reversal of fortune theme, and the survival of the unfittest theme.*

Sample Analytical Paper Topics

II. The picaresque theme
   A. Dante lost in Canto I
      1. In woods
      2. Midway on way of life
      3. Right road lost
   B. Approached by form
      1. Says Dante must go another way to leave a wasteful life behind
      2. Says Dante should take him as guide
      3. Says must pass through an eternal place and terrible peril
   C. Reaction of Dante
      1. Asks Virgil to lead him
      2. Follows behind

III. Reversal of fortune theme
   A. At beginning of *The Inferno*
      1. Alone
      2. Lost
      3. Dark
      4. Woods
   B. Appearance of form
      1. No longer alone
      2. Will serve as guide
      3. Morning rays of sun
      4. Now at base of mountain
      5. Will allow Beatrice to take over later in the journey

IV. Survival of unfittest
   A. Dante threatened from beginning
      1. Lost

2. Three animals
    a. Leopard
    b. Lion
    c. Wolf
  B. Dangerous journey
    1. Specters along way
       a. Demons
       b. Giants
       c. Dis
       d. Others
    2. Environmental hazards
       a. Fire
       b. Ice
    3. Weight of live person
       a. Dangerous on rocky paths
       b. Dangerous in boats
  C. At last emerges and sees stars

Topic # 2

Dante tells his own story. Do you think an objective narrator could have presented his story better than Dante, who was close to the story? Explain your answer.

Outline

I. Thesis Statement: *Dante tells his story more accurately and with more emotion and feeling than an objective narrator might. He is familiar with the time frame, the settings, the characters, and his own feelings and emotions.*

II. Time frame
  A. Has lived through the events
  B. Can present time accurately because present

Sample Analytical Paper Topics

      C. Can relate time frame to that of Christ's crucifixion and resurrection

III. Settings
- A. Actually found self in woods
- B. Actually tried to climb mountains
- C. Understood caste system in Hell
- D. Actually experienced each circle and area of Hell
- E. Actually experienced the contrasts among emerging from Hell, dark woods at beginning, and Hell itself

IV. Characters
- A. Actually saw the leopard, the lion, and the wolf
- B. Actually spent time with Virgil
- C. Saw and talked with many characters in Hell

V. Feelings and emotions
- A. Could describe some of them well since had experienced them
- B. Remembered feelings of fear, anger, sadness, and loneliness
- C. Portrayed feelings and emotions honestly—even the ugly ones

Topic # 3

Many conflicts are evident in the *Inferno*. Conflicts can be person-against-person, person-against-self, person-against-society, and person-against-nature. Which of these conflicts do you think exist in the *Inferno*? Explain your answer. Be sure to include examples.

Outline

I. Thesis Statement: *In Dante's* Inferno *there exist all four types of conflict: person-against-person, person-against-self, person-against-society, and person-against-nature. These conflicts are evident as Dante observes those within the Circles of Hell; Dante himself experiences these conflicts.*

II. Conflicts experienced by shades in Hell
    A. Person-against-person
        1. Count Ugolino
            a. Remembers Archbishop Roger
            b. Remembers being imprisoned by Roger
            c. Remembers children and self starving to death
        2. Archbishop Roger
            a. Condemned Ugolino in life
            b. Eaten by Ugolino in Hell
    B. Person-against-society
        1. Simon of Troy
            a. Lying Greek
            b. Convinced Trojans to bring wooden horse inside gates
            c. Conquered their people
        2. Master Adam
            a. Falsified coins
            b. Made money off society
    C. Person-against-nature
        1. Cold affecting those in lower realms
            a. Ugolino in cold area
            b. Frozen eyes of Ugolino
        2. Punishment by demons, centaurs who are twists of nature
            a. Kept in boiling river
            b. Pricked their skins with arrows

Sample Analytical Paper Topics

      D. Person-against-self
          1. Noise from those in Vestibule
          2. Unable to make a decision
          3. Rush aimlessly about and never make a commitment
III. Conflicts experienced by Dante
      A. Person-against-nature
          1. Lost in dark woods
          2. Sees leopard, lion, and wolf
      B. Person-against-society
          1. Experienced political parties in life
          2. Exiled because of beliefs
      C. Person-against-self
          1. Had to struggle to control emotions
          2. Had to struggle to stay on right road
      D. Person-against-person
          1. Conflicts with Virgil
              a. Dante's showing sorrow for sinners
              b. Dante's watching conflict among sinners
          2. Conflicts with sinners
              a. Becomes angry when sinner tells him fate of Guelphs
              b. Demands to know names of sinner

Topic # 4

Writers use many devices to reveal the main character to their readers. They may show the character in action, reveal the thoughts of the character, show what the character says to others, show what others say to the character, and show the character in various environments. Which of these devices does Dante use to expose himself to his reader? Explain your answer.

Outline

I. **Thesis Statement:** *To reveal himself completely to his reader, Dante shows himself in action, reveals his thoughts, shares what he says to others, shares what others say to him, and presents himself in various environments.*

II. Shows himself in action
   A. Stumbles back when confronted by the wolf
   B. Cries at plight of sinners in the beginning of his journey

III. Reveals his thoughts
   A. Concerned when guide is angry with him
   B. Despair and overwhelming terror when confronted by the wolf

IV. Shares what he says to others
   A. Asks Virgil to have pity on him
   B. Tells Virgil there may be a kinsman of his in Circle VIII
   C. At times speechless

V. Shares what others say to him
   A. Advice given him by Virgil
      1. Told by Virgil not to take thought of who is there
      2. Told by Virgil not to stare at those shades in conflict
   B. Told by shade of the blow to stagger the Whites

VI. Presents himself in various environments
   A. Frightened in woods
   B. Tries to climb mountain but cannot
   C. Misled by towers which are giants' legs
   D. Confused as to whether going up or down during exit
   E. At mercy of guide on journey
   F. Angry at shade who tells him fate of Whites
   G. Distressed at plight of shades

SECTION FOUR

Bibliography

Quotations from Dante's *Inferno* were taken from the following translation:

The Comedy of Dante Alighieri: Cantica I: Hell. Translated by Dorothy L. Sayers. New York: Penguin Books, 1949.

In addition, Sayer's introduction was indispensable to this study. The following works were also consulted often during the course of this work:

Ayearst, Morley. "Divine Comedy," *Merit Students Encyclopedia.* Chicago: Crowell-Collier Educational Corporation, 1969, p. 28.

Bergin, Thomas. "Dante Alighieri," *Encyclopedia Americana.* Danbury, CT: Grolier, Incorporated, 1989, pp. 487-490.

Bergin, Thomas. "Dante Alighieri," *Merit Students Encyclopedia.* Chicago: Crowell-Collier Educational Corporation, 1969, p. 444.

The Divine Comedy of Dante Alighieri: Hell. Translated by Henry F. Cary. New York: P. F. Collier and Son Corporation, 1957.

Kunitz, Stanley and Vineta Colby, "Dante Alighieri," *European Authors 1000-1900.* New York: H. W. Wilson Company, 1967, pp. 210-212.

Lambert, Walter J. and Charles E. Lamb. *Reading Instruction in the Content Areas.* Chicago: Rand McNally Publishing Company, 1980.

MAXnotes® are simply the best – but don't just take our word for it...

"... I have told every bookstore in the area to carry your MAXnotes. They are the only notes I recommend to my students. There is no comparison between MAXnotes and all other notes ..."
– *High School Teacher & Reading Specialist, Arlington High School, Arlington, MA*

"... I discovered the MAXnotes when a friend loaned me her copy of the *MAXnotes for Romeo and Juliet*. The book really helped me understand the story. Please send me a list of stores in my area that carry the MAXnotes. I would like to use more of them ..."
– *Student, San Marino, CA*

"... The two MAXnotes titles that I have used have been very, very useful in helping me understand the subject matter reviewed. Thank you for creating the MAXnotes series ..."
– *Student, Morrisville, PA*

"... [MAXnotes] provide perspectives I had never thought of, helpful questions, and practice essays I find myself using again and again. This series is simply the most helpful and concise tool I have ever found..."
– *Teacher, Joshua Tree, CA*